Suicide and the 90-Day Window:

How Spirituality, Metabolic Health, and a Service Dog Can Save Your Life

Mary
The good Lord has a plan. Trust
Him to move to the light.

Arn & Raider

Arn Manella, KM

BA Psych, MS Systems Eng

First published in October 2023.

Formatted by Sean Donovan www.Seandon.com

Cover Photography by Carmen Tate

ISBN: 9798863286907

Imprint: Independently published

Printed in the United States of America

Disclaimer

I am not certified in any medical or psychological practice. Any information on diseases, treatments available, or dietary considerations is intended for general information only. It must never be considered a substitute for the advice provided by a doctor or other qualified healthcare professional. Always seek the advice of your physician or other qualified healthcare professionals with questions regarding your medical condition. At any time and at my sole discretion, I may change or replace the information in this book. To the extent permitted by mandatory law, I shall not be liable for any direct, incidental, consequential, indirect, or punitive damages arising from access to or use of any content available in this book, regardless of the accuracy or completeness of such content.

Contents

Praise for *Suicide and the 90-Day Window*

America is a nation that is not healthy. Physically, spiritually, or emotionally. First responders suffer from living in this culture, with the added burden of being on the front lines of the consequences. I have worked in Fire and EMS since 1993 and never imagined I would see young people die with the frequency I do today. Meanwhile, our workforce is less and less prepared to handle the societal carnage they see. It should be no surprise that suicide kills more first responders than line-of-duty deaths, and the number of people needing long-term absences to deal with mental health issues is growing. I believe *Suicide and the 90-Day Window* has a real chance to help those at the point of the unthinkable.

Arn tackles his suicidal ideation like a Marine, bringing overwhelming force to bear. First responders will easily relate to Arn's life as a doer, the mistakes that play over and over in his head, his multiple careers, and his honest assessment of life and work successes and failures.

Around the firehouse table, we share stories; this one will inspire and educate those suffering. It will feel familiar and show that improvement is within reach. No magic pill. It takes the same problem-solving attitude we use every day in our jobs. Arn inspires us to get after it and shows us an approach that recognizes the whole person.

- Captain Agee Bryant, Henrico Fire, Henrico, Virginia

###

Arn Manella's own confrontations with the demons of Post Traumatic Stress and active suicidal ideation have provided useful tools and insights that will help many veterans (and others) who should read **Suicide and the 90-Day Window**. Arn's experiences are graphically real-life and clearly applicable. He has not returned from the pit of despair with empty hands. This, his report, deserves a wide readership."

- Gerald W. Scott, Ambassador of the United States

I would like to invite you along on one man's fascinating journey toward mental health. I first met Arn many years ago when he was a soccer referee assessor. I owned a pro team, and he would be at most of our games. When he would assess referees, many would quake in their shoes because Arn had a reputation for "ripping their lips off." As we moved along in life, the two of us had a youth soccer referee camp. I had to constantly keep an eye on him to not lose his cool with the kids. Two other referees were helping with the camp, both retired Marines. They both admitted to me that they were actually terrified of Arn.

All of this happened because Arn was in a bad place. His beloved wife had passed away, he was having problems on the job front, and his PTSD was rearing its ugly head.

At this time, he turned to the church. Popular opinion was that he felt safe there (which is not bad). I think it probably saved his life and helped him to make the decision to turn his life around and seek to be healthy, happy, and fulfilled.

For me, watching his journey has been both painful and inspirational. From working for the Sheriff's Department at an airport before, during, and after 911, working in Emergency Management during hurricanes, flooding, an active shooter incident at a government building very close to my office, and counseling the survivors of the shooting for two and one-half months after the shooting, I would have loved to have *Suicide and the 90-Day Window* with me in my pocket!

Most people don't realize that those who work in Emergency Management are under constant pressure – hashing and rehashing past events, practicing for future events, and responding to current events. The pressure is always there because an entire city or state is counting on them to make the best decisions to protect the citizens.

Suicide and the 90-Day Window is a good start to educating the public as it is very relatable. Our society needs more discussion and education on this topic. Most people don't realize how many people have personal trauma that leads them to thoughts of suicide. I now work with the mentally ill under temporary 2 detention orders, and almost all of them have some trauma that has led to thoughts or attempts at suicide. I wish I could get *Suicide and the 90-Day Window* in their hands. Because of all Arn has been through, his willingness to share, and his remaining a kind, loving, and helpful person, I am proud to call him a friend.

I would like to leave one thought – it came from the TV show "Castle." "Even on the worst day, there is the possibility of joy."

- Cookie Ketcham, MA in Counseling; Clinician III, Emergency Services Unit, Virginia Beach Department of Human Services

###

"Arn's story serves as a lesson to all who have served our country. *Suicide and the 90-Day Window* is a must-read not only for veterans but for active-duty military and First Responders and their families. Arn weaves vital information regarding suicide and PTSD throughout his own life story making for compelling reading. I've known Arn for over twenty years and I never knew the struggles he faced in dealing with his demons. Anybody who has faced danger and death and survived while losing comrades can relate to Arn's personal tale. I highly recommend **Suicide and the 90-Day Window.** The insight you will gain could help you with friends, family, buddies, or yourself in facing issues of PTSD and suicidal thoughts."

- **Captain Dave Huffman, Norfolk Police Department (ret)**

Healthcare and military forces often seem diametrically opposed or, at the very least, strange bedfellows. Military action will undoubtedly necessitate an increased burden on healthcare providers, both mentally and physically. Where military action requires a dehumanizing mindset to allow for effective action and force used against another human to preserve the safety and liberty of others, healthcare focuses on the innate 'spark' in every human life, forgoing feuds, tribes, and differences to help each uniquely designed individual at a time. Yet, despite the seemingly opposing nature of these forces, underlying the individual operator's drive, motivation, and sacrifice remain the same: to protect, support, preserve, and restore others without regard to one's safety and comfort.

This sacrificial spirit is shared by Service Members and healthcare providers, police, first responders, and many others. In all cases, the actual or perceived 'power' to impact another human's life requires extreme mental focus, emotional control, and an unwillingness to accept failure to be successful and respectful of the authority that society has collectively placed on these individuals. Unfortunately, this unwavering focus on others carries an exacting mental, emotional, and physical toll.

Fortunately, this toll also binds our communities together in support and strength.

As a Veteran and doctor myself, I have been honored over the years to be able to serve my fellow Brothers and Sisters in Arms both while serving on Active Duty and now in private practice. However, I had yet to learn what was in store for me the first time I met Arn.

Before long, our planned 30-minute appointment lasted 90 minutes as Arn, and I discussed his history and experiences; his research for his book *Suicide and the 90-Day Window* revealed that many dentists report moderate to high stress levels at work and medium to high levels of depression. Demonstrating our shared focus on the value of every human we encounter.

I am extremely honored to have been able to observe as Arn put together this excellent Field Manual, which will undoubtedly provide the support and guidance needed by many who either struggle with or know someone who struggles with PTS, depression, and suicidal ideations. It is a must-read for all who share in the profession of sacrifice.

- CPT Alexander Vaughan, USA, Ret; DDS, Virginia Total Sleep

###

I have known Arn for six years, and I have always enjoyed his insight. What is never realized was some of the struggles that he was experiencing. In *Suicide and The 90-Day Window*, Arn has opened his deep inner self to us so that we can understand how suicide and suicide ideation are affecting our veteran population at its core. According to the Veterans Administration, in 2020 there were 16.8 suicide deaths among veterans per day. While I have not suffered from suicide ideation, I have several veteran friends with whom I served in the Navy and the Marine Corps who committed suicide. By Arn opening himself up to us and sharing his inner struggles, *Suicide and the 90-Day Window* has given me insight into the sufferings of those who have served our country, and it has helped me to understand how I can assist my fellow veterans – no matter how long they served – to see that there is hope. I recommend *Suicide and the 90-Day Window* to every veteran or to anyone who has a relationship with a veteran so that we can reduce the pain and suffering that is hidden beneath the surface.

-Chip Souser, US Marines

###

In *Suicide and the 90-Day Window*, Arn Manella shares a harrowing yet inspirational account of his battle with suicidal ideation during his life and career in the military and public safety. His journey through the darkest corners of his mind is not just a personal testament to resilience and courage but a beacon of hope for others facing similar struggles.

Arn's raw honesty permeates every page, laying bare his inner demons and the significant adversity he faced both professionally and personally. His story resonates deeply, particularly for those who have found themselves trapped in the dark pit of despair, fighting against the urge to give in.

As a retired law enforcement officer, an attorney, and someone who has lived a life full of various challenges, I found myself profoundly connected to Arn's story. His battle with active and passive suicidality mirrors my own experiences. I felt an overwhelming sense of solace in knowing that someone else had not only endured similar struggles but triumphed over them.

Arn's multi-faceted approach to healing—encompassing physical wellness, spiritual growth, radical honesty, and the support of others—provides a practical blueprint for others in their own battle with mental health. His willingness to seek help, combined with a determination to keep pushing, exemplifies a method of overcoming adversity that doesn't promise overnight success but rather a gradual, steadfast path to recovery.

From the perspective of a former Police Officer, peer, Crisis Negotiator, Special Operations Supervisor, Chief of Police, and now a supporter, I wish I had a resource like this earlier in my career and life to offer others actively dealing with suicidality or attempting to understand it to help someone else. *Suicide and the 90-Day Window* fills a much-needed gap in understanding and combating one of mental health's most complex and challenging aspects.

I highly recommend *Suicide and the 90-Day Window* to anyone seeking insight, inspiration, or solace in the struggle against suicidal thoughts or mental adversity. The profound impact of Arn's words will undoubtedly reach many hearts and minds, encouraging those who feel lost and alone to keep fighting and pushing on.

In a world where one may feel so distant from understanding and empathy, *Suicide and the 90-Day Window* serves as an echoing voice of companionship, reinforcing the importance of community and faith. My profound gratitude goes out to Arn for making me feel heard and understood at a time when such feelings seemed almost unattainable.

"Do not be conquered by evil but conquer evil with good." (Romans 12:21). Arn is a living testament to this Biblical truth, a gentle reminder that even in the darkest of times, hope, perseverance, and faith can lead us towards the light.

- Charles P. Bowles, IV, Attorney, Chief of Police (ret.)

Foreword

In August of 2022, I was a chaplain for the Order of Malta Annual Pilgrimage to Our Lady of Champion Shrine, located near Green Bay, Wisconsin. One of the pilgrims I had the pleasure of meeting was Arn Manella, accompanied by his faithful service dog Raider. I got to know this remarkable man, who told me of his service in the United States Marine Corps in Vietnam and his ongoing challenges in dealing with Post Traumatic Stress Disorder (PTSD). I served eleven years as a chaplain in the United States Naval Reserve. Having spent time with sailors and marines, I became more aware of the difficulties many service members can experience in dealing with the harsh realities of combat and loss.

Arn Manella's testimony on how he has successfully dealt with and continues to deal with the trauma he experienced is outlined in a very readable way in *Suicide and the 90-Day Window*. You will feel that you have entered into a friendly conversation with Arn once you start reading it. Arn tells his life story with great honesty and hopefulness.

In the Marine Corps, the troops are taught the importance of obeying orders. They are also taught that when a situation changes, they must "innovate, adapt and overcome." This spirit of meeting new challenges head-on is how Arn lives his life. He sets forth the many strategies he has adopted to find meaning and balance in his life. Arn's devotion to God and the Catholic Church are front and center in his explanation of how he has found peace.

Since we are all created by God, it makes perfect sense that turning to Him in the midst of our difficulties is not simply a "coping strategy" but rather the necessary step for understanding why we are here on planet Earth and what we are supposed to do with our life.

Arn has led a fascinating life of devoted service to God, country, and family. His concern for those going through what he has experienced led him to write this wonderful account of what God and he have done together to overcome tragedy.

His message to all of us is that life is a beautiful gift from the Lord, and He will guide us if we say yes to that gift each day of our lives.

- Fr. Gerald E. Murray, Magistral Chaplain, The Sovereign Military Order of Malta, Pastor, Church of the Holy Family, New York, NY June 2023.

- Father Gerry is a commentator on religious topics on various television and radio outlets, including EWTN, EWTN Spanish, Fox News, Fox Business News, MSNBC, NY1, Radio Maria, Fox News Radio, and the Voice of America.

Introduction

In a room of one hundred people, close to one hundred percent will know of someone who has committed, attempted, or told them personally that they have no reason to go on living. Any suicide, a friend, sibling, significant other, or God forbid your child, leaves you with the question, **"Why?"**

Is there something you could have done to stop the tragedy? Is the pain so great you are actively or passively considering suicide yourself?

My goal is to offer realistic avenues you can travel should suicide present itself on the horizon; approach it prepared and leave it in the rearview mirror. I will describe my actions and the therapies I've used to move from active to passive suicidal ideation.

Using myself as the guinea pig, I will take you along on my journey, revealing "How I" am negotiating the many speed bumps and potholes that continue to hamper a safe exit from the active suicidal ideation highway toward my ultimate destination of living a happy, healthy, and fulfilled life.

Together, we can ***Move to the Light!***

Chapter 1
Overview

A Second Career, a Third, a Fourth...

I served twenty-three years in the Marine Corps. Although most of that time is chock full of cherished memories of past successes and accomplishments, there are private moments when I need to find a dark room, sit alone, and cry.

Many say combat is **"months of boredom punctuated by moments of terror."**

For veterans with combat-related PTSD, I would rephrase that quote. **"PTSD is months of passive suicidal ideation punctuated by moments of active suicidal ideation."**

Following my retirement from the Marines, I struggled to find employment. I couldn't hold a meaningful job providing for my family and self-interests.

I was a headhunter for a worldwide employment agency. Then I was a recruiter with one of the nation's top-tier insurance companies. Next, I was a Special Police Officer with a municipality where I worked in the environmental crimes arena. And following 9-11, I returned to my DoD roots serving as Intelligence Analyst in Mid-Atlantic Maritime Infrastructure under US Joint Forces Command.

In every instance, although I received awards for performance, I found myself dissatisfied with a work environment where higher-ups encouraged profit or blind obedience while sacrificing respect for the employee. I lost the job for being too dogmatic, expecting too much from co-workers, bristling when my integrity was questioned, being too honest, and being a workaholic.

I'm sure many of my fellow veterans can relate to this situation in the civilian world, and you can appreciate I was out of work a lot. Unfortunately, this instability is one of many shortfalls resulting in my divorce from a fantastic lady.

To put food on the table and rescue my self-esteem, I turned to various part-time employment where my physical conditioning, focus on attention to detail, and instructor skills are showcased. Among these are a Professional Soccer Official and Assessor and, again, returning to my military roots, Director of Intelligence and Scenario Development for a Law Enforcement Training company.

Coping with PTSD in my daily life

For years, I ignored when physically hurt, and while maintaining a tough exterior, I became mentally broken inside. Still, the outside world saw me as just fine. I denied obvious indications that I needed help.

One of my greatest pleasures is certifying top-level sailors to be competent instructors. In a proactive self-protective measure, I tell the instructor candidates that I will demonstrate examples of an instructor's positive and negative traits during the period of instruction. In reality, I protect myself against uncontrolled, inappropriate outbursts that I know specific triggering scenarios and/or candidate comments will surface.

When tact didn't satisfy my goals alone, I returned to showing the outside world an image of the rugged Marine. If you still don't get the point, I'd threaten to "Rip your lips off." Knock me down, and I'd get right back up. And always willing to "take one for the team." Sadly, that attitude has not proven to be the wisest choice.

As I said, it cost me my career, my wife, and, until now, the benefits I am likely due.

Benefits...are not a gift...you earned them.

Why has the benefits issue come front and center? It's simple. I have decided to live a long time, and it's about time; I've earned these benefits and need them to live: Happy, Healthy, and Fulfilled!

- I can't be happy if I cannot assist my family, friends, church, and other veterans when needed.
- I can't be healthy if I can't do those physical and mental things that are the two key pillars that support the archway of Fulfillment.

Many highly rated programs are geared toward veterans, law enforcement, first responders, and their families outside the VA system. On January 17, 2023, in response to the unacceptable daily 17 veteran suicides, the VA instituted The COMPACT Act, a program for ALL veterans in acute suicidal crisis. This covers veterans within and outside the VA system and is at NO cost to the veteran.

Along the road to healing, I've completed all programs offered at the VIP Center at McGuire VAMC in Richmond,

Virginia, including acupuncture, biofeedback, and Tai Chi, to name a few. But, in the final analysis, Mindfulness is the most beneficial.

Soft-Core Suicide

I will cover the growing threat I call Soft-core Suicide and offer a doable remedy that may improve and save countless physically and mentally damaged lives related to dietary considerations and participation in activities that pose a potential risk.

Most importantly, the effect of what you eat and drink can move you from an apparently normal day toward brain fog, a sense of uneasiness, and depression in a matter of days, if not hours.

Research: Personally and unscientifically conducted.

To better understand my PTSD, over the last decade, I've conducted an unscientific survey of over one hundred veterans with PTSD or Borderline Personality Disorder (BPD). The least functional share similar traits:

- Single-family home
- Considered a loner or "strange" in school
- No competitive sports or organizations such as Boy Scouts or Girl Scouts
- Joined up to change their life
- Lack of belief in God

Highly functional veterans are nearly the opposite; they joined in service to Our Country and believed in God.

To underscore the increased focus on the issue of veteran suicide, the Veterans Administration, National Institutes of Health, peer-reviewed medical and psychological journals, and periodicals on PTSD have gone from a few hundred twenty years ago to hundreds a year today.

###

Companion animals are better than any drug.

Another area I've found beneficial is companion animals. Most folks think of small animals like dogs and cats, and I have both. But my long-time love is horses. I've had a horse throughout my childhood and into adult life. The emotional tie to a dog is excellent, and the relationship with a large horse is powerful.

###

Remaining active is critical.

Divorce final, I moved out of the house and onto my sailboat for the next decade. Life was fine, and I was within walking distance of the PX, Commissary, and Church. However, once my daughter told me she was pregnant, "through the tunnel and onto the boat," it didn't seem inviting. So, I sold the boat and purchased a historic house and property circa 1793. Hah! "Over the river and through the woods, to grandfather's house we go!" has a much better ring. Don't you agree?

Still, I lived alone and had too much time on my hands. Without a steady 9-5 job, if it wasn't for attending daily Mass and the periodic soccer and sailing assignments, I had plenty of time to think dark thoughts.

Another avenue is creating a **YouTube** channel, **"MajorWortzNall."** Initially, the channel covered topics I found interesting: **"R U a Fat Head or a Fat User?"**, **"Planning to Die...Happy, Healthy and Fulfilled!"** and **"A Marine admits...He's a coward"** and three videos on the Coronavirus **"Coronavirus Opportunity,"** **"Coronavirus and Old Folks,"** and **"Covid-19 Is It Really All That Different?"** These last three videos created in mid-2020 proved to be sufficiently contentious amid my growing list of subscribers, YouTube, and some family members; consequently, I ceased adding additional videos to MajorWortzNall.

I joined a yacht club to fill the gaps, dusted off my metal detector, resurrected writing my factional book and poetry, began hiking, and went on a pilgrimage in Europe.

Beware of trying to save everyone else.

All of the above modalities provide both positive and negative aspects. It's okay when I realize I may spin out of control and prepare beforehand. The downside is opening myself to a relationship, be it as a mentor or a friend, especially when that relationship ends in their suicide.

Spirituality and Religion are possible factors for survival.

Although I recognize that suicide is ever present in my mind's deepest region, it's anathema to all I believe in. And that's the key takeaway. You must believe in more than just yourself. You must know there's much more about life than your daily grind.

Please remember, this is my journey, and it's been a Godsend.

That said, do your homework, work with your primary care physician (PCP), spiritual advisor, or priest, and make an honest effort to receive your earned benefits.

AND NEVER GIVE UP!

God bless you one and all.

Chapter 2
A Deeper Dive

There is no argument that the number of suicides in the USA and globally is rising rapidly, especially among two categories: young adults and veterans of the armed services in roughly the 15 to 40 age group.

Combat-related PTSD damages a veteran in ways the general public cannot readily recognize, such as losing a limb or disfigurement.

My situation didn't parallel many of my fellow Marines serving in Vietnam. Instead of an infantry unit, I was assigned to a service group "in the rear with the gear." And although death sometimes did stare me in the face, the most severe daily threat to me was a sunburn.

My assignment is to a Special Services Recreational Unit as a lifeguard on the beach. A job included: general lifeguard duties, certifying others to be lifeguards, and teaching folks how to swim. That last category encompassed many: fellow servicemen who learned to swim in a pool but not the ocean, civilian contractors, and Vietnamese children from the local hamlet.

Your students will often form an attachment with the instructor and vice versa. In this specific case, one of my younger Vietnamese female students was killed by Viet Cong in reprisal for her family consorting with the American occupying forces.

Initially, when I found out, I was hurt and sad. But, over the next few days, I began personalizing her death. I had many pictures of the kids swimming, receiving their swimming certificates, and enjoying cake and fruit juices at the celebration. Duplicates were sent home with the kids and proudly displayed in their hootch. Could these pictures be used to identify which kids and adults were "fraternizing" with the Americans? Am I responsible for her death?

Now you may be thinking, how can I make such a leap?

First, it should be evident that I was not responsible, and that should be that. And, in retrospect, I can agree with you.

Yet, in context, the combatants' death is chalked up to the hazard of warfare, but the end of an innocent's life can lead to irrational thinking and behavior. Thus, the second seed of my considering suicide is sown.

The first seed is months earlier on the plane, taking me and some forty recruits from Chicago to California and the Marine Corps Recruit Depot, San Diego. Eddie and I sat together on the five-hour flight and discussed what we did before joining the Marines. We found we had a similar background, Boy Scouts, competitive sports in high school, and Catholic. We were fast friends and both Marines when we finished boot camp.

As luck would have it, my first assignment after the Infantry Training Regiment was a six-week school at Quantico, Virginia. I was going to learn how to store and transport munitions safely. In addition, I received an introduction to identifying and disarming mines and booby traps.

Eddie got a plum assignment to a year-long communications school in California.

Before we departed for school, we had thirty days of boot leave to show off our new Marine uniforms, use expletives not appreciated by family, and do our best to burn the candle at both ends.

Going immediately to Vietnam after Ordinance School, I spent my initial thirteen months lying to Eddie about how dangerous my life was and how he was such a coward resting on a beach in California.

With the hope Eddie and I would be in Vietnam simultaneously, I extended for an additional six months. Eddie received orders to join a unit just north of me near Da Nang. I received permission to travel there and meet up, only to find he was on a ship I could see leaving the harbor.

As the math worked out, if I extended another six months, we might still meet up, or, better yet, we would be returning to Chicago at nearly the same time. I would arrive about ten days before him. Boy, did we have plans!

I was home shy of a week when I returned to my house at three o'clock in the morning. All the lights were on. I entered. My mom and dad are sitting in the front room. They told me Eddie was dead.

A few days later, and dressed in my green Service Alphas, I escorted Eddie's coffin to the funeral home. And, as I entered, I nodded to those gathered, and Eddie's sister held me, and we cried.

Eddie's mom turned into the room. Then, looking me straight in the eye, she said, "Why not you?"

I knew she didn't mean it then, but today the question remains. So, for the next fifty-five years, I have been haunted by that question.

Those incidents are the first and second seeds in my garden of life that should contain sunshine, lollipops, and rainbows, but instead, are choked with the darkest nightmare weeds, bitter ashes, and an empty, rusting pot that should have contained gold.

The specter known as PTSD waits patiently until I decide suicide is the only response to Eddie's mom's question, "Why not you?"

Today, I am rated by the Veteran's Benefits Administration to be 90% disabled due primarily to Combat-Related PTSD and related Obstructive Sleep Apnea (OSA) and considered 100% totally disabled and individually unemployable (TDIU). Additional "traumatic seed-bearing" situations have existed throughout my Marine career and civilian life.

###

Since 2009, I have participated in many therapies and programs to reduce the probability of becoming a suicide-related statistic. Although I have found many answers in the clinician's room, I can genuinely say I can best understand what I am going through in the waiting room among fellow veterans.

###

The most critical period for someone considering suicide is the first twenty-four hours.

If the veteran has access to a quick means of action, such as a firearm, there is a higher probability they will succeed.

Each of these methods: poisoning, cutting, hanging, or even suicide by cop, takes more planning and follow through to be successful except for hanging. Here the neck may break, or slow strangulation occurs with the person discovered in time—leading the veteran into the maze of professional help.

Often, the individual considering suicide goes from immediate suicidal ideation to action, failing that, a period of depression leading to unsuccessful attempts, or hopefully, a recognition by the veteran or family and friends that there is a deeper problem, and they need help.

I call this the **90-Day Window**. My research into suicidal ideation reveals approximately a ninety-day window of opportunity between contemplating suicide and survival.

If you drew a line representing these ninety days, it would not be straight. It would be a bell-shaped curve. The first four days following a traumatic incident appear the most critical. The individual believes there is no other way to cope with the situation than to end it.

Yet, once the individual recognizes a problem or willingly accepts family, friends, or medical professionals' counsel, the therapeutic programs are many and usually run for twelve weeks.

Once in a program and as the days pass, the impulse to commit suicide diminishes.

The individual reaches a critical point when approaching the top of the curve.

In my case, here I am; the initial trauma, while not extinguished, is submerged deep enough that it's no longer front and center. Still, the slide down the curve results in a mental roller coaster.

Just as a roller coaster will add sharp turns, dips, and dark tunnels to increase excitement, this coaster adds a new twist; it separates into two sets of cars now on different tracks.

One set of cars leads away from suicidal ideation toward hope for the future.

The other represents intervention, say, a particular mental health clinician or a VA program, Cognitive Processing Therapy (CPT), Prolonged Exposure (PE), and Eye Movement Desensitization and Reprocessing (EMDR).

Nearly full stop at the top of the curve, the cars rush toward the end of the ride.

The expected outcome is that the cars will eventually slow down until gently nestled into their respective bay. That is how the ride is supposed to end.

But what happens if one set of cars doesn't slow down as expected?

What if the individual faced with the scheduled end of the intervention panics?

Without confidence, something is in place to mitigate the crash; the individual might move, in a heartbeat, from passive to active suicidal ideation.

###

Although I was initially an enlisted Marine, I received a commission and rose to selection for Lieutenant Colonel. In my last eleven years of duty, I served as a Strategic Intelligence Analyst, primarily in the terrorism arena. In addition to attending the National Intelligence University's (formerly the Defense Intelligence College) Post Graduate Intelligence Course, I have a BA in Psychology from Chapman University, Orange, California, and an MS in Systems Management, from Viterbi School of Engineering, the University of Southern California, Los Angeles. Thus, research and finding the answers is a passion.

The thought of committing suicide is ever-present, but I am a Marine, my belief in God is unshakeable, and the decision to change my path led me to the Nutritional Ketosis lifestyle.

When I decided on the Keto lifestyle change, it was directly in response to a realization I was rapidly entering a danger zone of bad decisions, what I now call Soft-Core Suicide. Living alone, I had few folks around me willing to tell me something was wrong. My primary care physician said all my markers were within recommended limits. I did have HBP (145/98), chronic sleep apnea, my drinking remained problematic, the weight could improve (247 lbs), and there is that nagging PTSD thingy. My doctor's prescription, keep walking and watch your diet, and everything should be fine.

Fine! Now, what did that mean?

Was it fine that I was a hermit except for going to church? Was it fine that I couldn't hold a 9-5 job because I didn't trust my supervisors and fellow workers, or I was prone to outbursts at the drop of a hat? Was it fine that my drinking became the glue holding each hour of each day together? A pattern of drinking so structured that if I missed my weekly sojourn to the ABC store, I would receive an email from them asking if I was OK.

Was I OK? No, I wasn't OK! I was falling deeper into depression.

Depression.

Years earlier, at the Veterans Medical Center, McGuire in Richmond, Virginia, following my initial diagnosis of PTSD, I took part in many programs offered to reduce anxiety and depression. The VIP center is excellent. The modalities available run the gambit from Acupuncture to Zen. I tried them all. To further "assist" in my recovery, Zoloft becomes the answer.

I had difficulty finding a full-time job, so most jobs were part-time and seasonal, either in the professional soccer or sailing arenas. In addition, I'm a novelist. Each job requires me to be sharp, make split-second decisions under pressure, and create believable characters or situations. Unfortunately, as the Zoloft kicked in, I became too chill on the water, less critical of a referee's performance, and my characters resembled cardboard cutouts rather than action figures.

Over some time, higher-ups nudged me out of professional soccer, and my novel **Merchant's List** languished.

###

A Road Map to Mayhem

In 2009, while accompanying my Marine son to Long Beach, CA, VAMC, for his treatment (he is 100% physically disabled), I agreed to take an online survey for PTSD. The result: ***"Seek professional help immediately."***

Returning to Virginia, I had my semi-annual physical at the Richmond VA Medical Center (RVAMC), Richmond, VA, and I intended to tell my primary care physician the survey results. Before my revelation, she said her staff assignment at RVAMC was ending, and she would return to Johns Hopkins. It took me a long time to develop this trusting relationship, and the news hit me hard. I broke down, relating how I used the five-hour flight back from California to make a list of possible causes for my PTSD. I spoke about Vietnam, Pakistan, Africa, and other venues where the multiple situations I encountered contributed to the problem. Recognizing my critical state, she went down the hall and returned with immediate consultation with a clinician in the PTSD clinic. Recognizing once I departed her office, I'd head straight home, she took me by the hand to the clinician. That, as they say, is how I have arrived at this point in my struggle.

The following list includes specific situations in my career where the environment and actions I've taken or witnessed directly impacted, over time, the severity of my PTSD.

Let's start with my I arrival in Vietnam in June 1966

- A decision is made to obliterate a Viet Cong stronghold. I assisted in placing explosives in bunkers, tunnels, and civilian hootches. **Comment**: Seeing the civilians forcibly removed and the probability some remained in

16

the tunnels became a problem and didn't help win their hearts and minds.

- I was reassigned from the Ammo Dump to Lifeguard duty at the beach. Received training in Saigon and was designated Water Safety Instructor. **Comment:** At one time, I certified all lifeguards in the I Corps military region. An added bennie in Saigon is attending a one-day US Army class on underwater mines and booby traps. I already had similar training when I attended Ordinance School at Quantico before arriving in Vietnam.

- Working with the Marine Combined Action Team, I taught local Vietnamese children to swim. **Comment:** Several months later, one of my students, and her family were killed by the VC for consorting with the Americans. Also, several VCs killed in our area were members of the volleyball team we played regularly.

- The beach is closed most of the monsoon season. **Comment:** I volunteered to stay busy as a unit courier, usually flying on a Hu-ie. I received OJT as a door-gunner. Often went on contact patrols or provided security for convoys resupplying units. On occasion, we returned with injured Marines, some KIA.

- In recognition, I was promoted from L/Cpl (E-3) to Sergeant (E-5) by mid-1967—a total of sixteen months of active service.

- My best Marine buddy Eddie and I joined; he was assigned to Comm School after the Infantry Training Regiment and wouldn't graduate for many months. I continually wrote to him and, at one point, called him a coward. As it would happen, with my acceptance to Marine Security Guard School and Eddie's end of a tour with 3rd Tracs, we would be home at about the same time. **Comment:** Eddie was KIA ten days before returning home. Upon seeing me, when I went to his funeral, his mom asked, "Why not you?" I stood next to his casket the three days of the wake.

Returning stateside and beyond

- I attended **Marine Security Guard School (MSG)** less than three months later. **Comment:** I dedicated my training to Eddie. I graduated **Honor Man** of my class. Assigned to the **Special Security Detail (SSD) Department of State, Office of Diplomatic Security, and designated Special Agent.**
- Assigned to **AmEmb Rawalpindi, Pakistan**. **Comment:** A thrown brick hit me in the head during the riots. Ambassador ordered no documentation in the official record, confiscating MSG's side arms and shotguns, stating, "I'll not have Marines killing anyone!" I provided security for the visit of President Nixon to Lahore.
- I am assigned to **AmEmb Pretoria, South Africa.** There I met my wonderful wife.
- Accepted to the **69th Officer Candidate School** and returned stateside to Quantico. **Comment:** Commissioned a 2nd Lt (11-70).
- During the **Evacuation of Saigon. Comment:** I was responsible for securing the aircraft carrier flight deck and directing arriving Vietnamese evacuees. At one moment, I find myself flashbacking to the destruction of the VC hamlet nearly a decade earlier. Awarded **Commandant of the Marine Corps Certificate of Commendation.**
- I am assigned as the **Marine Corps Staff Assistant to the Code of Conduct Review Committee. Comment:** My duties include conducting the pre-brief and

debriefing of POWs testifying before the Committee. Once the POW arrived, I would review the process (relax, let everything out since there would be no record of testimony, etc.) and relate my father was a POW during WWII. In one case, the former POW took off his shirt and showed me and the Committee members the nearly two hundred cigarette burns placed on his back and legs by North Vietnamese Army guards. As I debriefed individual POWs in a secluded office, we often cried. Awarded the **Joint Service Commendation Medal** for distinguished service in a joint duty capacity.

- I held several billets in **Pacific Command, Camp Smith, Hawaii,** including Terrorism Analyst. One of my highlights is the first-ever Aircraft Hostage, no notice exercise by the US Army "Blue Light." **Comment:** The "Blue Light" force is the precursor to today's Delta Force. The next day, on Kaua'i, now in my role as Terrorism Analyst, I witnessed the arrival of "Blue Light" and the hostages' rescue. Some "hostages" likely suffered from the ordeal, even after realizing it was only an exercise. This event is among several noted when the Navy League recognized me as the **Pacific Command's Junior Officer of the Year.**

- Iranian Hostage Rescue Attempt. **Comment:** As Terrorist Analyst and my high-level clearances, another analyst and I are assigned to monitor all-source information and raw communications during the run-up to the order to execute and awarded my **second JSCM** for distinguished service in the terrorism arena.

- **US Central Command, Terrorism Analyst/Member of the Anti-terrorism Survey Team. Comment:** Our mission: is to assist US Diplomatic Missions and Military installations in our command's Area Of

Responsibility (AOR). Assistance is in the form of on-site security evaluation/recommendations, and preparing necessary documentation in support of Non-combatant Evacuation Operations (NEO). Also, my duties included, but were not limited to, assessing the "credible" terrorist threat in that particular location/region and, when necessary, traveling to/embedding with US (Delta/SEALS) and friendly SOF (British SAS, etc.) in direct action collection operations. For these and associated actions, I received the **Defense Meritorious Service Medal** in recognition of distinguished service by non-combat outstanding achievement.

- Our team is scheduled to fly into Karachi, Pakistan, on the Kuwaiti flight from Frankfurt to Karachi via Doha, UAE. In Frankfurt, a US official directs us to fly instead on a Pakistani International Airways flight to Karachi. Upon our arrival in Karachi, we learned our original Kuwaiti flight was hijacked to Tehran. **Comment:** Later, we are told that terrorists assassinated a US Diplomat on that flight. We also learned the source document specifically identified our team leader by name. No wonder he always wanted to room with me.

- Arabian Peninsula. **Comment:** During a diplomatic "meet and greet," a case officer informs me that the US Diplomat assassinated in Tehran was a long-time personal friend. Based on what he knows, he says that the real target was one of our team members. I was stunned by his verbal abuse. He went on, "You guys get paid to die. My friend was a guy selling the region corn and rice." Then, he struck me.

- **Overall Comment:** When taken in total, the sheer number of bodies and mutilations observed, inserts into hostile areas/actions, and verbal/physical abuse from foreign nationals, US government officials, and civilians has, over time, led me into a very dark place.

So, why am I hesitant to report myself to my commander, or at least medical officers, and ask for help? In retrospect, I can see a similar reluctance to self-reporting because I am looking to retain my position on the "team", and, in addition, looking forward to obtaining employment in the civilian sector upon retirement. An entry in my medical record identifying emotional distress could be a career-ender. And, indeed, that's also a concern of others trying to protect me, though now I see that it was misguided. Hindsight is often perfect.

You're off the Team

"You're off the team if I report this," said the medical officer.

Those few words likely not only sealed my lips but also sealed my fate. Up to that point, I believed I could continue to carry out my duties without admitting I was under severe emotional stress.

The "team" the doctor refers to is ostensibly named the Anti-terrorism Survey Team. This four-person team, tasked with evaluating the security environment for military and diplomatic posts throughout the US Central Command's area of operations, typically operates independently. However, on occasion, it can be augmented with US Army or USN special operations personnel depending on whether the mission is feet dry or wet, sometimes both.

The senior officer is a highly decorated, no-nonsense pitbull Army Ranger Colonel. The Navy Medical Officer Lieutenant Commander and USAF Tactical Air Major also provide critical infrastructure knowledge. As the Marine Intelligence Officer terrorism analyst, I identify credible terrorist threats focused on the specific mission area.

On this most recent deployment, our team was identified by regional bad actors, who directly named our team leader and threatened to impede or neutralize our effectiveness. They hijacked a civilian aircraft we should have been on and executed the US Government personnel aboard.

On the flight home, I had ample time to ruminate upon the possibility our team might have failed to survive this mission. I immediately sought to relate my concerns to the medical officer, resulting in him counseling me but not entering my mental condition in my service medical record.

In retrospect, this was not the first instance where circumstances put me and those around me in harm's way. Each time I brushed it off as just part of the job. I didn't want to tap out of the situation. I kept ignoring that I needed help. Sadly, the support available followed a sliding scale from a few days off to some powerful medications. I flushed the meds down the toilet. I had to remain in control. But was I?

Through my close relationship with the Special Operations Forces (SOF) while on active duty and now in retirement, I've come to appreciate the pressures of the job. This pressure is present not only among the service members themselves but also their families. There is a likewise pattern among Law

Enforcement, Fire, and First Responders and, surprisingly, in the medical professions.

###

The decision to commit to a highly dangerous and emotionally draining endeavor requires that the individual and the profession commit to early recognition of the individual's condition and follow-on clinical support.

###

On Suicide and Image

I ran my first marathon in November 1976, the inaugural for the Marine Corps. At the time, I considered myself in pretty good shape and set a goal of finishing in about four hours. A leisurely pace, to be sure. I read many books on running and knew at some point, say eighteen miles, I'd hit "the Wall," and I did. I finished closer to five hours and was among the last to cross the line.

That was over four decades ago.

On a dreary, drizzly Wednesday, February 5th, 2020, I hit another wall, the "WALL." The Vietnam Veterans Memorial in Washington, DC.

I made a *Major WortzNall* video in honor of my Marine buddy Eddie. In preparation, I took tracing paper and charcoal to rub Eddie's name and a container of Brasso. A flag pole at the Wall has the service emblems in brass at the base. I aim to polish the Marine Corps emblem until it outshines them all.

As I knelt at the emblem and set to work, a tear fell with each circular stroke. After a few minutes, a volunteer at the Memorial came over to see if I was OK.

No, I wasn't OK, and I wondered if I would ever be, as I recounted for the thousand times Eddie's mom's "Why not you?"

We sat on a nearby bench, and I told him Eddie's story. He listened, and I sobbed as quietly as possible. Again, he asked if I was OK. I hesitated for several moments. And I asked myself the same question. Thanking him for listening, I gathered up my gear. The tracing paper, charcoal, can of Brasso, and rags went into my pack. Into my heart and mind, the mantra "Why not you?"

The drive back to the farm takes just over an hour and meanders along country roads with sparse traffic. With each mile, I relived my actions at the Wall and the closer I came to the farm, the closer I came to giving up.

As luck would have it, sufficient miles are available to plan how I would do it.

Key points to consider:

1. I must retain my image. I am supposed to be of strong mind and body and have many accomplishments.
2. I do not want folks second-guessing how it could happen and why.
3. I do not want my family burdened with the stigma that suicide brings.
4. Therefore, it must be seen as a terrible accident to keep my image intact.

The last fifteen miles to the farm, and as I wind down Highway 721, I am greeted by oncoming traffic and somewhat closely by eighteen-wheeler logging trucks. I drive a Mazda. If I am struck by an oncoming passenger car, there is a high probability that both drivers will die, and I wouldn't want that to happen—but being hit by a logging truck. Well, I have little doubt death would be instant. I am sure the drivers of these rigs, especially on two-lane roads, are trained to stay the course when a minor obstacle, say a deer, a tire tread, or a Mazda, suddenly obstructs their path. Suicide by a logging truck and no one the wiser. Just a terrible accident. I am gone, but my image remains.

As I pulled into the driveway at the farm, I saw Raider bounding down the front porch stairs, his tail wagging out a welcome home semaphore message of love. Typically, as soon as I turned off the engine, I'd open my door, and Raider would jump up and shower me with kisses. Today, I just sat there. Who else is waiting for me to return so they can welcome me home and hug me closely? As I ponder these thoughts, Raider sits quietly, and his head tilts slightly as if to ask if something is wrong. Yes, something was wrong. At that moment, I realized how selfish the action of taking my own life would be, and I needed help.

The next day I contacted the mental health clinic at McGuire.

Chapter 3
Getting Help

I have resisted getting help for my combat-related PTSD from the beginning of my symptoms as early as Vietnam. Here's my rationale.

1. I never thought I had a problem.
2. I considered complaining about being a wimp.
3. I figured I could always force my emotions down.
4. I see veterans at the VAMC who need help more than I do.
5. I believe being in control is still the best policy.

By following my approach, it cost me the following:

1. My career.
2. My marriage.
3. My respect among family and friends.
4. My failure to receive the disability benefits I've earned.

###

Receiving the benefits I have earned.

Since my retirement and after I entered the Veterans Administration medical system at age 65, I hesitated to use the benefits I had earned. Sure, I signed up for annual physicals, used the pharmacy for most prescriptions, received blood work, and used an array of X-rays and therapies when necessary. For the most part, I wasn't much about complaining. A key driving force keeping me from submitting any claims is that as I walked the halls of the VA, I couldn't help but notice how many veterans were in pretty bad shape. I'm not just talking about being overweight; it's the number of wheelchair users, amputees, and those requiring assistance just to get around. At this time, I had not entered into the mental health system.

Armed with a referral to the Mental Health Clinic and preparing for the appointment, I methodically searched for as much information as possible on combat-related PTSD. And when I mapped out all the variables, I accepted I was a classic case needing professional intervention.

Initially, I saw a nurse, a psychiatrist, and a social worker. Encouraged to participate in group counseling and individual therapies such as acupuncture, biofeedback, and mindfulness, I jumped in feet first. To arrest a tendency to overreact to trigger points, I am prescribed Zoloft. Lastly, the BSN suggested I contact the Disabled Veterans of America (DAV) service representative and see if they can help me file for disability.

At the DVA local chapter, I was teamed up with a Marine, and we set about documenting my case and submitted it for consideration. The result came back, rating me at 30% for combat-related PTSD. The formal notification also noted I had missed a Compensation and Pension (C&P) examination. Based on the information in my current claim, a completed C&P exam could likely result in a higher rating.

Until then, I wasn't receiving anything, so the 30% paid for my liveaboard boat slip. I may have been happy, but my problems were just beginning.

I used my research background to begin the process, and you can too.

The first step is to visit: **https://benefits.va.gov/benefits/**

If you haven't previously been to the aforementioned website, create an account.

From there, just follow the prompts. Such as: Apply for VA Benefits and Disability Compensation. It's all very straightforward.

There are a lot of questions, and most are easy to answer with the access you now have at your fingertips. Build your case with military health records, secure buddy letters, and testimonials from previous/current employers.

###

The **NEXUS Letter** is critical to your disability claim. It's essential to locate a medical professional that understands the military mindset and has access to your military records. In my case, Dr. Frank fits the bill, and as a personal friend, he has observed me in both private and public settings.

Key findings:

Member has an occupational and social impairment, with deficiencies in most areas,

1. Work, family relations, social relation
2. Mood, due to such symptoms as suicidal ideation; (Finally accepted help after years of denial)
3. Near-continuous panic or depression affecting impaired impulse control (such as unprovoked irritability with periods of violence);
4. Difficulty in adapting to stressful circumstances (including work or a work-like setting);

5. Inability to establish and maintain effective relationships at work and with family and friends. My professional opinion is that his inability to hold meaningful employment since retirement from active military service is more likely than not directly connected to his existing combat-related PTSD.

Since my retirement from active duty, I have served as an instructor for advanced trauma life support for the American College of Surgeons and Instructor ████████████ In addition, I serve on staff in the emergency department ████ ██

Frank ██████ MD FACEP CAPT (ret) MC USN

Comment: Dr. Frank's letter summarized my situation nearly three years ago. If not a total basket case, I would have been close to it. I had just begun daily clinical interventions, increased my physical fitness regime, and, in consultation with my PCP, began following a ketogenic metabolic therapy. Here's the rub. Except for family and one or two close friends with whom I had constant contact, the outside world saw me as just fine.

Outwardly, I demonstrated an in-control, unyielding personae credited to my Marine exterior and bearing. Inside, I was struggling to keep it all together.

###

If the NEXUS Letter is essential, the Compensation and Pension Exam (C&P exam) can be critical. Once you've filed a claim with the U.S. Department of Veterans Affairs (VA) for disability compensation or pension benefits, the VA may ask you to undergo an examination as part of the claim process.

Once again, the key is for the examiner to have a complete picture of your military history and medical record. Be honest with the examiner and do not embellish or leave out pertinent information.

The following is an excerpt from my C&P exam. Dr. John immediately made me feel comfortable as he commented on my Marine career, commands and operations, and medical record. The examination took nearly one hour, and I was emotionally drained at its conclusion. 4

█████████████████████████████

Key findings:

He reported conflicts regarding how he exposed fraud or other unethical practices and suffered repercussions as a result. However, the sum total of his temperament and behavior was consistently described as preventing him from maintaining a job on a full-time basis. Treatment notes from █████████████ dated 7/10/20, indicate veteran's thought processes were more impaired and his insight into the effects of his behavior on others was impaired to the point of being distorted in two directions. One limiting his awareness of how his behavior was viewed by other people, and the other being the pattern of rigid and catastrophic thinking that would lead him to behaviors that others would find more assaultive than he was able to comprehend.

He reflected on the past and his experiences in Vietnam that he had forgotten until applying for benefits. He continues to struggle with thoughts about being responsible, although he is able to realize he is not completely responsible for certain events and others' choices. 2

###

Just because you hit above the 30% disability rating, if you have additional service-connected injuries, or illnesses-follow up. I am currently in the benefits claim process for Toxic Waste exposure under the **PACT Act**. Why am I pursuing this additional illness you might ask?

###

Another option is the Veterans Readiness and Education (VR&E). The VR&E program helps Veterans and Servicemembers with service-connected disabilities and an employment handicap prepare for, obtain, and keep suitable jobs. It is authorized by Congress under Title 38 of the United States Code, Chapter 31. It is sometimes referred to as the Chapter 31 program. Most recently, I approached the VR&E folks about assisting me in entering the William and Mary M.ED in Counseling. I am drawn to this program because the Military and Veterans Counseling specialization within the Clinical Mental Health Counseling concentration responds to the critical shortage in counselors and clinicians by training culturally (military) responsive counselors who are prepared to address the unique behavioral health needs of active-duty military personnel, veterans and military-connected families. But, as often happens, I was turned down by VR&E because they said my Service Connected Disability (SCD), combat related-PTSD disqualifies me from the counseling Masters because of comments made by my clinician indicating there are concerns about my ability to interact with, work alongside, and sustain a full-weeks of effort.

Oh well, maybe not the hill I'm willing to die on, but I will seek out other options.

All this VA-related assistance is good, and it goes a long way toward getting me on the right road to recovery, but I must be willing to help myself. And there are numerous techniques available. I mentioned earlier that, of all the programs I completed at the VIP Center at McGuire, Mindfulness is the most beneficial. I can take it anywhere. It's always available when I find myself heading into a dark tunnel to clear my mind and get me back on the right track.

Mindfulness-what was old is new again.

In November 2016, I was invited by Dr. Elizabeth A. Stanley, Ph.D. Associate Professor of Security Studies Georgetown University and Army veteran to participate in a VA-sponsored conference on the use of Mindfulness as a possible treatment for service members before and upon return from combat who may have PTSD. The training was offered at the Omega Institute in Rhinebeck, NY.

The Institute presents itself as *"More than simply a place, Omega is a global community that awakens the best in the human spirit and cultivates the extraordinary potential that exists in us all."*

Following the weekend event, Dr. Stanley held a five-day "information class" of selected individuals to highlight the effectiveness of the Mindfulness-based Mind Fitness Training (MMFT) program in pre-deployment preparation for military personnel assigned to a combat environment. Another benefit is that some in the class may be selected to participate in follow-on training to join her cadre of MMFT instructors. Lastly, she and her staff would observe us and ensure those selected would be a "good fit."

Due to my previous background in Mindfulness training and combat-related PTSD, I believed I was a good fit for the team. When I didn't receive an acceptance letter for several weeks, I emailed to ascertain my status. When I did receive a response from Dr. Stanley, it stated bluntly I was not fit for the team because she and her staff assessed me as "disordered." I was disappointed that I was not selected. At the time, I chalked it up to just another opportunity lost.

I know now this pattern spans decades.

Early in the seventies, one of my initial assignments was as Director of the Challenge and Development Center (CDC) at Camp Pendleton, CA. The residential center focused on returning Marines caught up in the recreational drug use web to full duty. I was removed from that assignment for using mindfulness as a treatment.

Here we are fifty years later, and Dr. Stanley is contracted to present similar training to deploying Marines.

In preparation for my CDC assignment, I attended several programs at universities and institutes. The University of California, Los Angeles, Medical School's two-week program for Drug and Alcohol-Related Issues. The University of Oklahoma, Norman Medical School's two-week program on Adolescent Drug Use and a program held in the Big Bear Lake area of California. My attendance at these programs was not without detractors. Soon after Vietnam and in the military, I sometimes found myself in a hostile setting. At the Big Bear facility, I was greeted by a gauntlet of tambourine banging, guitar playing, antiwar singing, and Patchouli oil-smelling greeters, several of which beat on my car, and one even spit on my windshield.

Fast forward to 2016, turning onto the entrance of the Omega Institute, I was greeted by a similar, though less antagonistic, gauntlet. Still, with the guitar playing and singing, I had to pull into a shaded area, turn off my engine, and chill. The flashback to Big Bear was that intense.

I did gain a lot of valuable information and established solid contacts I could use when I returned to Virginia. Authors Peter A. Levine *"Waking the Tiger"* and Thich Nhat Hanh *"Taming the Tiger Within"* both made presentations and motivated me to rekindle my interest in Mindfulness.

Using Jon Kabat-Zinn's eight-week Mindfulness-Based Stress Reduction (MBSR) training as a guide, I crafted a similar program titled *"Mindfulness and the Catholic Church."* Each session begins with a 10-minute centering activity focused on mindful breathing. The ensuing lessons cover Silent prayer, Lectio Divina, Imaginative prayer, the Examen, Asking for Grace, etc. The goal of the training is to bring the parishioner into a state of mind where they are completely absorbed into their prayer life and, ultimately, fully aware during the Mass. All other distractions are gently moved aside, leaving them truly at the foot of the Cross in company with Our Lord Jesus Christ, His mother, Mary. Mary Magdalene. Mary of Clopas. and John, "the disciple Jesus loved."

Sharing this with you is my way of connecting the dots in my military and civilian career, pointing to why my battle with active suicidal ideation is being won. By remaining connected with reality and accepting the assistance of medical professionals, family, friends, and God, I can live a happy, healthy, and fulfilled life.

Chapter 4
Soft-core Suicide

Soft-core Suicide is a term I've coined to identify a person neglecting how their dietary decisions directly affect their physical and mental issues, resulting in reduced quality and length of life. Over time I have found some specific practices crucial in living my life: Happy, Healthy, and Fulfilled.

Still, intending to live a long life happily, healthy, and fulfilled can have a downside.

The longer I live, I find myself burying family and friends at an alarming rate. The passing of my mom and dad is, to be sure, a sad event. No longer will I have their sage counsel or undying love to comfort me, and although my brother and I had many run-ins, I miss him. These losses can be expected.

One of the most tragic events that can happen to a parent is to bury their child.

###

Aside from war, there are numerous reasons a child may pass early; one is a disease. The disease can be planned for and offers time to spend with the loved one. Another is an accident that, although not planned, offers some closure.

There is the possibility that a veteran on active duty in either training or combat could lose their life. When we talk about first responders, law enforcement, and firemen, they are dangerous professions, and the possibility of death is always present. Less understood is the suicide of someone in a field not generally associated with danger: medical, financial, and sports professionals.

Regardless of the reason, suicide takes life in an instant.

When suicide happens, it tears the survivor's emotions apart because it's not only the loss of the loved one's life; it's the continual re-examination that something they did or didn't do is the cause of the death.

The possibility of suicide, where the indicators exist, can be mitigated. But when it's a soft-core suicide, that's what upsets me. And in my specific case, it is entirely in my hands to prevent it.

In the United States today and likely globally, type 2 diabetes (T2D) is prevalent among adults over 45. Children under the age of eighteen are rapidly approaching the adult percentages. Type 2 diabetes was not an issue until it got on the radar in the late 1950s and early 60s. So, what changed?

What changed is the food pyramid.

My mom had a set menu for the week when I was growing up in the 1950s and 60s.

- ➢ Monday is hot dogs.
- ➢ Tuesday cube steak.
- ➢ Wednesday hamburgers.
- ➢ Thursday, smoked pork butt, a big favorite of mine.
- ➢ Fridays are fish days. Everybody was happy, well I should say.
- ➢ Saturday is cornmeal, or, as we say, clean out refrigerator night (CORN).
- ➢ Sunday, of course, growing up in an Italian family, is pasta. It could've been spaghetti, bow ties, ravioli, or

lasagna. My mom made the best lasagna in the entire family. And, always meat, usually big meatballs or sausages.

The week's menu centered around beef. When I visited my aunt, liver and onions were always on the table. I drew the line at Grandma's pig's feet.

In the early 60s in high school, I remember the food pyramid displayed in the cafeteria. The food pyramid had beans, veggies, cereals, rice, whole grains, chicken, and fish but only a little red meat. When I asked the cafeteria staff why there was no meat menu, they said the USDA Dietary Guidelines indicate that red meat is dangerous for your heart. Well, as it turned out, when Americans started eating the Standard American Diet (SAD) and stopped eating red meat and eggs, substituting low-fat dairy, and turning to margarine instead of butter, you can almost point to that as when type 2 diabetes becomes an issue.

Keto, Suicide, and Image

In the spring of 2016, I volunteered to enter a four-year nationwide VA-sponsored study hosted by the Georgetown University Memory Disorders Program, looking into a possible correlation between Vietnam-era veterans diagnosed with PTSD and the onset of Alzheimer's. The study included: cognitive assessments, blood draws, spinal fluid draws, MRIs, PET scans, and experimental medication. After an informal discussion with the staff and mentioning the difficulty with my writing, I was cautioned against using Zoloft and statins. Taking that information back to my VA Medical Center, I spoke with my psychiatrist and PCP; we agreed to stop Zoloft and statins and monitor the situation. Another concern of the program staff was 3 my weight and my current diet's physical and mental adverse side effects. Although they didn't specifically suggest Keto, it was apparent that at least one staff member is a believer, not only because of the weight issue but if I committed to that lifestyle change, it could significantly reduce my alcohol use. I tucked that information away.

It was Fall 2018, and my waist was expanding outward alarmingly. My doctor recommended fewer calories, increased workouts, more vegetables, polyunsaturated fats, fruit, and whole grains. I listen to him, and my waist continues to expand. In August 2019, I set a moderate course to remake my life. I wanted to bolster my faith, exercise my mind and body, and escape. So, I organized a three-week pilgrimage to Scotland. I've always had an affinity for Scotland—especially the fine single-malt whisky. I grew up in an Italian family (my dad's) with a smattering of Belgian culture (my mom's). For the better part of seven decades, the Italian/German connection was a particular part of who I am. My son purchased DNA tests for me, my daughter, and him as a Christmas gift. I'm pleased to report that I am Scot, Irish, and Welsh, with a Belgian touch.

Hah, the love of single malt surfaces!

The first week I spent on the Isle of Iona. The weather was perfect, the connection with early Christianity solid, the food fantastic, and the beer and whisky superb. I walked, climbed to the highest point on the Isle, Dun I, at 101 meters, or 333 feet, and played matador to a giant bull stationed outside the entrance to the Catholic Prayer House where I stayed.

In the second half of my journey, I traveled first to Inverness, then up to the Northlink Ferry at Thurso, and across to Orkney and a week-long pilgrimage along St Magnus' Way. Once again, I ate, walked, and drank my way around the island. Unfortunately, although everything was positive for my increased faith, my waist 4 stayed relatively the same, and I had an excruciating encounter with the Stinging Nettle.

I returned home pumped up and in a better place, all being good until Christmas supper with my daughter and her family. I drank heavily and acted the fool, jeopardizing myself in the bargain. It wasn't pretty, and I was very embarrassed by my actions, especially in the company of my grandchildren. Ignoring my daughter's pleas, I left the house and drove the ninety minutes home to the farm. What an idiot and poor example. At that moment, I decided I couldn't continue like this and vowed to make a drastic change.

One of my pre-publication readers questioned "why" I'm providing so much in-depth information on my results with the Ketogenic lifestyle. My answer was that I could gloss over the facts and just say something like, "And I found metabolic ketosis therapy worked for me." But that's not emphatic enough. So, I include them in detail rather than pointing you toward the sources. I do the research, you enjoy the story.

So, I began my quest for answers; that's what I do. I'm a research analyst. I want to know the "why." And like any good

Intel Analyst, when asked to provide a decision-maker with factual information, I looked for at least three non-associated sources or position papers and "think" pieces that could point me in the right direction. I was sure all I needed was a different diet, and if I stuck with it, I could lose weight, so I dug deep.

I researched many diets: Atkins, the 30-day plan, Paleo, Weight Watchers, and the ketogenic diet; although Adkins was close to keto, it wasn't a lifestyle. A lifestyle change I believed I needed.

The information available on **YouTube** is astounding. I found Dr. Ken D. Berry, MD, Professor Tim Noakes, Dr. Eric Westman, MD, and Dr. Bret Scher, MD, whom I initially found when he was hosting **Diet Doctor** and, most recently, the **Metabolic Mind** podcast. I must've watched hundreds of videos covering low-carb/high-fat topics.

By Googling Keto, I surfaced peer-reviewed studies in South Africa, expanding to Australia, New Zealand, Ireland, and the United States.

An excellent way to determine the positivity of information an influencer is putting out on **YouTube** is to look at the number of subscribers. You are likely in the correct place when the general public supports someone who provides information that demonstrably improves their life. From the beginning, I saw Dr. Eric Berg, DC; he had three million + subscribers. Dr. Ken D. Berry, MD, is next closest, with just over two million.

As I researched the literature, it became clear that Keto was the way to go if I wanted to make the physical and mental changes I needed to live Happy, Healthy, and Fulfilled.

40

So, in addition, I created a **YouTube** channel: ***Major WortzNall.*** By doing so, I hoped to accomplish three things: 1. Establish an online support group. 2. Act the Guinea Pig cautiously, following the Keto lifestyle. 3. Surface problems attendant to someone in advanced years living alone and how to overcome them.

###

I spend a lot of time at the VA hospital; consequently, I often sit in the medical clinic and the mental health/PTSD waiting rooms. And what I see and hear is alarming. More than half of the veterans appear overweight and, in some cases, morbidly obese. When I talk to them, over 50% have type 2 or type 1 diabetes and the associated comorbidities. A good number also have cardiovascular disease. I make it a habit of not talking to them about what I eat unless, in the conversation, it becomes known that I am in my 78th and soon-to-be 79th year. They can't believe it, and when they ask, "How'd you do it? I'm only 60." That gives me an opening to discuss my ketogenic lifestyle.

Sadly, almost every veteran will tell me their doctors never discuss changing eating habits. Instead, they focus on fewer calories, exercise, eating more vegetables and cereals, and cutting out red meat and saturated fat; butter is terrible for you. Instead of butter, you should be eating margarine and using vegetable oils. And, of course...drugs.

Drugs. During my most recent visit to McGuire, I ran into a veteran I've talked to several times and hardly recognized him. Stretching his hand, he said, "I'm looking pretty good, huh?" And he was. I estimate he had lost thirty pounds. Curious, I asked what he had changed. I was shocked when he said **Ozempic®**. I was even more shocked by his remark when he said he hadn't changed much of what he was eating. His doctor said he is pleased by the weight loss and the drop in his HBA1c from a high in the eights to the sixes. From what I can find in the literature on **Ozempic®**, he will have to continue taking the drug forever to maintain the weight loss. Once he stops, he will return to his previous weight and likely gain additional pounds.

And it's not his fault. Among many physicians, the common practice is recommending foods listed in the USDA Dietary Guidelines. When you look at what is recommended in the Standard American Diet (SAD), a low-carb/high-fat regime includes nearly everything that was either not discussed or considered dangerous to good health, especially coronary heart disease and diabetes. Not only is the Dietary Board strongly recommending no red meat, but it's also actively pushing toward vegetarianism.

Intermittent fasting

Another area I include in my lifestyle change is intermittent fasting. When I mentioned this to my primary care physician's nurse, she gave me a talking-to that had my ears burning. She said that fasting is very unhealthy and that you must eat three meals daily. Suppose you feel hungry in between... snacks. I'm living proof that my ketogenic lifestyle and intermittent fasting also work. And although some critics say keto is not sustainable, I've just celebrated my third anniversary.

What happens to the body when I don't eat for 24 hours? One is that if my body can't grab any carbohydrates to eat for energy, it goes after the fat already stored.

The most days I've spent on an all-water fast was five and coincided with the 15 days to "lower the curve" of the COVID-19 pandemic of early 2020.

So, what did I experience on the five-day fast?

On the first day and a half, I missed eating. Not because I was hungry but because I was out of my normal daily rhythm; by the third day, I was no longer thinking about food. I wasn't counting the hours or the minutes until I could start eating again; I saw the five days as an easily reachable goal. My brain function appeared way more precise than usual. Aches and pains have already significantly reduced because of keto have become almost nonexistent, and I just felt good. I lost twelve pounds. Of which, I gained back about five pounds in water weight.

Since then, intermittent fasting has become my daily regimen. I seldom eat more than one meal a day, and if I eat a second meal, it's generally within a four-hour window between 2 p.m. and 6 p.m. So realistically, I'm on a 20-hour fast from my last meal until my next meal. I feel great; I'm not hungry, and my food craving is nonexistent.

Expanding on Mom's menu

So, what am I eating?

Monday: that's going to be steak. I love a good ribeye, but I'll buy any steak on sale. Sometimes it's New York strip or flank steak, and often there's even T-bone. I like to go to Costco. I don't generally buy my meat there, though for the first time, grass-fed grass-finished ribeye. I see little difference in the taste.

Tuesday: Well, I'm only sometimes particularly eager to cook, so right after Mass, and at about 2 p.m., I'll go to my favorite Italian restaurant. The waitress knows what I'll request. First, Noel says, "OK, Arn, you're going to have a glass of Montepulciano." (a fine Italian red wine). Then, not missing a beat, I add, "Remember, if you see it below halfway down in the glass, bring me a second." Noel continues, "For the main course, you'll have a 12-inch Italian sausage sub with grilled peppers and onions, but no bun." I'm getting a big plate of Italian sausage. Now I do cheat a little bit on Tuesdays. I'll have a small side of French fries. I love French fries, which are my cheat meal of the week. Today is the only time I'll have something with starches; I know I will pay for it.

Wednesday; Liver. Once again, the Standard American Diet makes liver a big no-no. Today it's a big yes. The liver is a superfood and one of the most nutritionally dense. It contains vitamins A, B, folate, iron, and copper. Eating a single serving (3 to 6oz) of the liver can help you reach your daily recommended amount of all these vitamins and minerals, reducing your risk of nutrient deficiency. As I said, sometimes I dislike cooking, so I buy Braunschweiger. I make a big plate of half a pound of Braunschweiger, blue cheese, and mayonnaise. Yes, mayonnaise is good for you; it's primarily eggs. The only drawback is commercially produced mayonnaise, often made with soy oil. Therefore, I make my own by emulsifying eggs, oil, and some acid, usually vinegar or lemon juice. And I like large pork rinds. I spread the Braunschweiger on the pork rinds, a little blue cheese, and some mayonnaise. Fast and good. Almost every meat day is an avocado day.

Thursday: It can be steak; if I'm lazy, it's a cold plate of a pound and a half of Italian antipasto. Prosciutto, salami, Capicola and I'll add some hard cheese. If possible, find an antipasto that doesn't contain many preservatives. Generally, the cheese I like is Dubliner, which is very tasty.

Friday: My fish is going to be in three different types. First is a half-pound of wild-caught Norwegian sockeye salmon. Second, wild-caught sardines in water. Nice big fat sardines skin on bone. And one of my favorites... anchovies.

Saturday: It is steak day. A big, juicy pound and a half steak. I like to have my steak with Brussels Sprouts, though recently my skin itches when I eat them. And, if I can get them, escargot and avocado. The wine has dropped from a bottle to two glasses.

Sunday: One pound of wild-caught shrimp and a small bowl of pistachio nuts. And, that's it for the day. On occasion, I will end the evening with a wee dram of fine single-malt whisky.

I've been asked if eating so much meat is harmful. If I eat till I'm satisfied, that is the right amount. That said, a friend and I once ate a four-pound homemade cannelloni. We weren't hungry; instead, we were eating for the taste. Carbs can fool the brain. So, there you have it, mom's meat-filled menu with my choices added. I am glad I am winning the war physically and mentally because I want to live happily, healthy, and fulfilled.

So, is a nutritional ketogenic lifestyle sustainable?

I've closely monitored the changes over time; for example, in 2020 and my first six months of weight loss, I focused on limiting carbs and eating mainly meat. At some point between six and nine months, my weight plateaued. This was about the time when I went on a pilgrimage to Santiago.

I was in good shape, and I went out of my way to eat meat most of the time with some cheeses and wine, of course, and periodically I would have a desire for French fries. Within a week of my return from Spain, I was at the VA hospital for my semi-annual physical. I was so pumped that I thought after 36 days of walking, I would have dropped well below the 204 pounds I was when I left. When the nurse weighed me in, I was 212 pounds; I was pissed, but in retrospect, it was not just my total weight. Inches were gone, my waist went from about a 38 when I left to 36, and my strength and muscles, especially my legs, had increased. Hence, there was a difference; I had gained extra pounds of muscle.

Again, playing the guinea pig, I went on a 30-day no-alcohol trial and felt great. I had no desire to drink. I could look across my parlor and see a bottle of Macallan, a bottle of Red Breast, and then my 30-year-old Jura, but I didn't need alcohol. So, at the end of the 30 days, it wasn't like I needed to sit down now and make up for the lost time. Instead, I found it was nice to drink again, but instead of two glasses of wine with a meal, I could hardly get through one.

Following my no-alcohol experiment and to "celebrate," I joined my Malta friends at a local pub following our monthly St Francis Home visit. I ordered a pint of their Brown Lager and a plate of fish and chips. Then, wash it down with a second pint.

Later, back at the farm, I measured my Blood Glucose, 107. The following day it was 79.

What are the overall results of my 30 days without alcohol?

1. I slept better-6/7 hours
2. I felt clearer in mind
3. I lost 3 lbs
4. My skin is clearer

Going forward, I will continue to drink alcohol at a significantly reduced level. I do like the taste, especially with a good meal. I know this seems counterintuitive, and I agree. Most recently, during Lent 2023, I stopped all alcohol during the 40 days. I feel great, and there's a good chance I'll quit alcohol altogether.

In my estimation, there is ample evidence that eating the Standard American Diet is not a diet. It's a roadmap heading directly toward obesity, type 2 diabetes, coronary disease, and impaired brain function.

Then why are so many medical universities and dietary organizations pushing high carb, grains, seed oils, and low fat?

Occam's Razor, to paraphrase, says the simplest answer is usually correct.

As to the "Why?" I say follow the money. Many medical/dietary proponents of the high-carb lifestyle receive millions from big pharma and big food. Not just as institutions but individually. This is not me advocating a conspiracy. Instead, solid research identifies precisely who and how much they receive. And that is a violation of their trust.

The Hippocratic Oath requires a new physician to swear upon several Greek healing gods that he will uphold professional, ethical standards. The most basic being "first do no harm." Is it any wonder that doctors directed to, or through ignorance, prescribe the endless array of drugs and surgeries to heal a patient rather than first consider the most straightforward answer that may be moving away from the Standard American Diet?

Physicians are reportedly at a higher risk of suicide and suicidal ideation than the general population.

1 Shanafelt TD, Dyrbye L, et al. Suicidal ideation and attitudes regarding help seeking in US physicians relative to the us working population. Mayo Clinic Proceedings. 2021; 96(8)

In my experience, the ketogenic lifestyle is sustainable and lifesaving. Here are my stats when I committed to this life in January 2020:

Weight: 247 lbs

Complaints: Joint and muscle pain, brain fog, dizziness, irritability, tired, no energy, skin lesions, reaction to insect stings

Diagnosis: Rheumatoid Arthritis, Hypertension, Complex PTSD, Chronic Sleep Apnea, basal cell carcinoma, anaphylaxis

Meds: *Prescription*, Zoloft, atorvastatin, hydrochlorothiazide*, epinephrine (epi-pen) *Over the counter*: Aspirin, Tylenol PM, Aleve, diphenhydramine (Benadryl), Vitamin D3 (10,000 iu) and K2 (100mcg) *Pfizer recalled this drug because of elevated levels of potential cancer-causing impurities.

Here are my stats for August 2023:

Weight: 204 lbs

Complaints: Joint pain after I eat carbs and, or vegetables. Passive suicidal ideation, brain fog, poor sleep, and dizziness after eating chocolate cake and drinking alcohol.

Diagnosis: Keep doing whatever you are, but remain cautious around the chocolate cake and insects.

Meds: *Prescription*: Epi-pen, Lisinopril* *Over the counter*: Aleve, diphenhydramine (Benadryl), Vitamin D3 (10,000 iu) with K2 (100 mcg)

*I am challenging my PCP's decision that I need this hypertension-related drug.

UPDATE: I have a new PCP as of August 2023. She is really impressive. On our first meeting I was blown away that she made the effort to research ALL my medical history from active duty up to the previous six-month semi-annual examination. She said she's impressed with my improvement both physically and psychologically. Doc supports my ketogenic intervention and agrees there is no need for the BP meds. I am doing so well, she suggested we delay our next eval out to nine months. When I countered, I believed six months allows me to more accurately monitor my overall well-being, she agreed. Life is good.

My results, I believe, are due to my desire to find a non-pharmaceutical or invasive surgical intervention for previous physical and mental health complaints and the discipline to stick with it. As long as I know I am not alone and am loved and challenged daily, I can finally *accept that my PTSD IS a fundamental part of who I am, but I will NOT let it define who I can be.*

Therefore, I **CHOOSE LIFE!**

Chapter 5
Leadership, or Lack Thereof, Plays a Crucial Role

Are you trying to kill yourself?

On my way to a Boy Scout meeting, in company with an Eagle Scout, we heard a loud boom to our left accompanied by a concussion that rocked my van and spewed a large plume of black smoke into the air.

Agreeing it wasn't a BBQ, we turned in that direction arriving at a ranch-style house with fire engulfing the rear portion. We went to the backyard, where a neighbor tried to put it out with a garden hose. He said a Korean family lived there and was still inside.

I entered the kitchen, smoke and flame billowing from around the corner. Turning the corner, I nearly tripped over a man. I picked him up, and I got him outside. I had the Eagle Scout take sheets off a line, lay them on the man, and soak him with water. Speaking in broken English, the man said his wife and baby were still inside. I soaked a towel, put it over my head and shoulders, and returned to the house.

Flames and smoke were climbing up the walls toward the front of the house from the bathroom/bedroom area. Getting on my hands and knees, I crawled along the hallway and found the wife, her blouse and hair appeared badly burned. I got her out the front door and gave her to the neighbors.

I reentered to look for the baby. Not finding the baby, I exited just as the FD arrived.

They took over, put out the fire, and treated the Koreans and me primarily for burns and smoke inhalation. It turns out there was no baby. He meant "with baby" or pregnant. She did lose the baby.*

All clear at the house, the Eagle Scout and I continued to the Scout meeting.

Arriving at the event, we gave a short synopsis of our adventure. One of the more senior scouts said, "If anything like this were to happen, I'd expect Arn to be part of it all."

The meeting was over; I drove the Eagle Scout to his house and continued to mine.

It was a bit late, and the kids were already asleep. My wife was still up and reading in bed. As I stripped off my clothes and prepared to shower, I explained some 1 details to my wife. Then, without skipping a beat, my wife quietly but firmly says, "Are you trying to kill yourself?"

*For this action, I received the **Navy-Marine Corps Medal**. The highest military award for Heroism in non-combat action. Also, the BSA **Honor Medal** for demonstrating unusual Heroism and skill in saving or attempting to save a life at considerable risk to self.

###

In retrospect, that question, now forty years later, is finally coming into focus.

I've done much research these last three years on why a person considers suicide the answer to their problems. Money. Loss of a job or promotion. A sense of failure and not living up to expectations, whether theirs or others. Death of a loved one. End of a serious relationship or marriage.

Several months before the fire, I saw signs that my marriage was seriously in trouble. Until then, my wife and I had the usual spats and disagreements mostly centered around my inattention to, or unavailability for, special family events: my wife's birthday, the kid's programs at school, and our anniversary.

Everything took a backseat to my needs: my Marine career, soccer referee schedule, and Boy Scouts. My current assignment often requires me to be at work just after midnight returning home close to noon each weekday. My deployments with the Anti-terrorism Survey Team were often "no notice" and might run from a week or two to two months. Then there is soccer. To advance my grade as a referee, I attended training or officiated at matches once a weekday and often several times on weekends. My wife was outwardly supportive, and my son steadily advanced up the travel team ladder.

Boy Scouts was the only activity that encompassed the entire family. Initially, the troop was small, with only eight boys. In my youth, I also started with a troop of less than twenty, but once a dynamic Scoutmaster came aboard, within two years, the troop numbers were nearly one hundred and still growing.

With the training I received in that troop and Marine Corps, I was sure I could help the troop grow. My Central Command assignment wouldn't allow me the flexibility to take the position of Scoutmaster. As fortune would have it, another family with two sons also shared my opinion that new leadership is necessary. Jim's assignment at Central Command seldom took him away for extended periods. Jim and I were Marines and agreed the troop needed new blood.

Additionally, Jim is an Eagle Scout and best qualified to take on the Scoutmaster position. I was a Life Scout, and we agreed I should lead the Troop Committee.

Within three years, the troop grew to over one hundred, went camping every month, rain or shine, and attended the National Jamboree in Virginia and Philmont Scout Ranch in New Mexico. To keep the ball rolling, family members of the scouts were encouraged to serve on committees and visit the troop when we went camping. Although not a scout, my daughter is considered the best hiker for her age. My wife got into the mix serving as the Advancement Chair. Our Troop was a true family affair; it provided the glue holding the family and marriage together.

We were building a new home in Florida, and my dad was visiting and acting as the "unofficial" construction foreman. Dad had enough life experience to qualify as both an electrician and carpenter. The on-site foreman once said that Dad knew his stuff and wouldn't allow any corners to be cut. My dad often made suggestions that couldn't be argued with; besides, they liked Dad. Dad is also an excellent judge of character.

At a troop family gathering, Jim addresses the many accomplishments this past year and how critical family support is to the troop's success.

"This guy is a bullshit artist!" said my dad.

One evening at dinner, my wife and I argued in front of the kids. Recognizing its effect on them, we went outside and got into the van. The drive was nearly an hour long, and as we were rehashing the usual minor problems, I revealed that I knew Jim and she was meeting. At that point, she acknowledged that fact and said she wanted a divorce. Stopping the car on a quiet side road, I got on my knees and pleaded with her not to do this, asking if I could do anything to fix things. She admitted she still loved me. Before returning home, we agreed to try to salvage the marriage, but she added it wouldn't be easy.

The good news is that I'll be transferred within six months to my next assignment in Virginia Beach, Virginia, away from Jim.

The bad news, and as fate would have it, Jim gets orders to Norfolk, Virginia, two days before the house fire.

Was I indeed trying to go out in a blaze of glory?

My military career is full of fantastic opportunities to serve alongside truly outstanding fellow Marines and those in the joint service arena, yet some examples of poor leadership exist. Of course, poor judgment is one thing, but doing what appears morally wrong is a different story.

Earlier in my career, as a First Lieutenant, I was selected to work with Marines suffering from alcoholism, recreational drug use, and anger management. At the time, I was completing a BA in Psychology at Chapman University in Orange, California.

As a designated Human Relations Officer, I worked closely with Marines, and in some cases, their families, when the Marines had difficulty adjusting to state-side duty following combat in Vietnam. My accomplishments resulted in my receiving the **Navy-Marine Corps Achievement Medal** (NMCAM). In addition, I was transferred from my infantry battalion to the Division Staff as Director of the newly established Challenge and Development Center.

Initially, I successfully used some of the modalities suggested by my studies, earning a **Commandant's Certificate of Commendation**. I found Gestalt therapy for anger management and mindfulness successful across various issues. During a presentation to the Division Deputy Commanding General, I listed alcohol among the most destructive drugs abused. This seemed to unsettle the general. He went ballistic when I described our successes in the correctional facility with mindfulness techniques; he stood up, pointing at me, saying, "I'll not have my Marines turned into monks!" I was transferred from The Challenge and Development Center to the education office a week later.

During the evacuation of Saigon, I observed Vietnamese helicopters arrive aboard our carrier loaded with motorcycles, porcelain elephants, teak furniture, jewelry, and gold bars. Yet, at the same time, human beings were left behind.

I mentioned earlier that a key responsibility of the Anti-terrorism Survey Team is to assemble a Noncombatant

Evacuation Operations (NEO) plan used in an emergency action specifically outside the continental United States. Such a plan existed for Afghanistan and was apparently disregarded during the debacle of withdrawal from Afghanistan in September 2021.

This action remains a stark reminder that, even in the presence of credible information, leadership can make decisions that needlessly cost the lives of military and civilians alike.

Another takeaway is, "Why, if both wars ran for approximately twenty years, are the 58,220 KIA and 150,000 WIA in Vietnam so different? "

The simple answer is more than 90% of all U.S. military in Afghanistan survived due to the advances in trauma care.

###

On what proved to be my final active-duty assignment and during the Chief of Staff's (CoS) "Welcome aboard!", the colonel handed me a copy of an article authored by the Commanding General (CG) titled **"Never Trust Your Intelligence Officer!"** Over the next eighteen months, it becomes apparent that C.G. 's attitude hasn't changed since he wrote the article as a Lieutenant Colonel serving in Vietnam.

My previous four-year assignment with the U.S. Central Command allowed me to work alongside quality personnel from all branches of the military services and civilians. Consequently, I had access to information unavailable to Marine Corps operational units. For example, I knew one such Infantry Regiment Battalion deploying into harm's way would benefit by forwarding a detailed document I authored on the specific threat area. My counterpart in that regiment disseminated the paper to staff officers resulting in an "atta boy" message to my Chief of Staff.

You would think my command would be pleased, but the CoS said, "The C.G. reminds you that you are his asset, and you will not assist other Marine units without his express permission."

This is one of several examples where the information available to me is withheld, possibly resulting in casualties among U.S. and friendly third-country military. Administratively the general's position is correct, but morally not so much.

Be careful what you ask for.

There's a great scene in the movie *Patton* where Patton, played by George C Scott, is about to engage the great German Field Marshal Rommel, and as they set up the 6 tank battle in North Africa, Patton says, "Rommel, you magnificent bastard I read your book!" In this situation, knowing your opposite number is critical to your success in actual combat or an exercise. And coming out on top is all that's important.

So, as it happens, the C.G., before an upcoming exercise in Europe, asked if I could research any background on the commander of the opposing forces. I had many friends in the intelligence community and, due to my clearances, received a complete dossier on this specific commander. So I presented it to the commander. As he read its contents, he found that not only did it list the military schools and commands held, awards, and decorations, but it also revealed that when the commander traveled, he had a particular aid that traveled with him, and she was young. Well, my C.G., upon reading this, said, "I can't believe that we collect information like this on our friends." And I flippantly said, "Well, sir, I think you'll find they have a similar dossier on you. Is there anything you would prefer not known publicly?

Well, he threw me out of his office!

I've already mentioned Jim and his impact on my marriage, but I didn't realize how this negative mindset destroys my career. I approached him once I was convinced his relationship with my wife had progressed beyond casual meetings. I threatened to report him to his command for violating the Uniform Code of Military Justice Article 134 for Extramarital Sexual Conduct. The maximum punishment is a **dishonorable discharge, forfeiture of all pay and allowances, and confinement for up to 1 year**. Yet, he told me he loved my wife and would seek a divorce from his wife.

Not satisfied with his answer, I went to a good friend in the command who is also a military lawyer and laid out the story. His counsel was to consider how a dishonorable discharge would impact not only Jim's family situation but my family. The mental pressure on me severely hampered my ability to carry out my duties, although I did my best to press on. However, whenever I deployed, the image of Jim and my wife being together ate away at my inner being.

Finally, I decided to approach Jim's Chief of Staff. Both Jim and I served with the Colonel in my last command. When I suggested I wanted to press charges, the Colonel bluntly informed me that Jim held a position in the command critical to its mission. Therefore, it is doubtful that my "official" approach to "my" marital problem will result in the action I would desire. The Colonel told me to find another way because a trial would drag Jim, his family, and my family down and likely end my career.

Severely disappointed and determined to "work it out" the best I could, I just wanted to make it to the eighteen-month point in this assignment, retire, and focus on salvaging my marriage.

Three months before my separation date, as I sat in my office, I started having severe chest pains. I got into my car and drove to the base clinic. They immediately started taking my vitals and informed me they would transfer me off base to a local hospital with the appropriate personnel and equipment. The clinic staff told my wife, and she met me within the hour at the hospital.

As it turned out, the chest pain was likely due to anxiety. When I asked the staff if this was a normal stress reaction, they clarified that I was likely suffering from **Generalized anxiety disorder (GAD), usually involving a persistent feeling of anxiety or dread, which can interfere with daily life**. It is not the same as occasionally worrying about things or experiencing anxiety due to stressful life events—people living with GAD experience frequent fear for months if not years.

Gone are my career, marriage, and self-esteem all in ninety days.

###

My first full-time job in the civilian sector following retirement is as a headhunter with a worldwide job placement organization and an excellent opportunity to gain valuable experience in the real world. The pay is good; we draw $1,000 against future commissions at the start of each week. Simply this means the pay period we don't make a placement, the "draw" continues to add up. Getting your first placement can take up to ninety days resulting in you being already in the hole for up to $12,000. The key is finding a niche fast.

Due to my extensive military background, I knew a source of candidates in the Nuclear Power arena. I established the Nuclear Power Branch, and the placements began to fill in. After several months I was surprised my commissions weren't keeping pace with my draw of $1,000 a week. I went to my manager, who explained that any commission checks received by the Friday before a scheduled payday resulted in a commission. If the check isn't in hand, the commission is rolled over and reduced by the draw. He followed this up with, by the way, you are the **"Recruiter of the Month."** Congratulations!

Over time by redoubling my efforts, the commissions increased. I attended a going away party for a junior accountant, and as we were leaving, the honoree stopped me in the parking lot. She said she saw how hard I was working and wanted me to know that the standard procedure in accounting is to hold all placement checks received as early as ten days before payday and bank the check the Monday before payday. This manipulation of the published SOP on compensation effectively cheated the recruiter of commissions owed.

I returned to my desk and went through my past years' placement stubs and could see the difference in payout is significant. Taking this information to my manager, I was surprised he agreed with my findings. He instead indicated that he would review my payouts and increase any discrepancies. He cautioned that this was between the two of us.

Back at my desk, I emailed him outlining our agreement and asked if I had the particulars correct. Within minutes he responded in the affirmative.

I've previously mentioned how I often didn't think through the implications of my actions in a non-threatening environment. In this case, my knee-jerk reaction was that I took the email and the manager's response and shot-gunned it to every recruiter in the organization. As a result, a formal email from the company's owner informed me I was on notice as terminated within thirty days.

My wife had a very well-paid position with a corporate travel agency. Her clients were listed among the top 500.

So, I focused on two areas for the next several months to compensate for the shortfall. 1. Find a new full-time position, and 2. Accept as many part-time assignments in the soccer and sailing arenas as possible. The downside of both part-time jobs is they required me to travel up and down the East Coast, and I was gone a lot.

Taking my love for sailing to the next level, I started a not-for-profit, adaptive sailing program for sailors with disabilities. Initially, we had great local support, but the board of directors agreed that I needed practical experience with an established program with name recognition. At a Sail Expo gathering in Atlantic City, I'm interviewed by the manager of Shake-a-Leg, and I'm hired to be the head sailing instructor in Newport, RI. The season runs for about six weeks, and based on my performance, I'm asked to travel to Miami to direct the program. On the surface, this looks all good, but my absence provides Jim and my wife ample time to cement their relationship, and I agree to an uncontested divorce.

I remained with Shake-a-Leg for two years and returned home searching for a full-time position. I wanted to be with my two children, and although now divorced, I wanted to be nearby if needed.

A close friend in the soccer community informed me that the municipality had just posted a position for a Special Police Officer. And, based on my Marine training, I'd fit right in. I got the job and almost immediately realized I'd be most effective if I remained clear of my senior supervisor and in the field. Over the next few years, our interactions were limited. Although I was rated as outstanding and promoted twice during my six-month reviews, I am cautioned about being too dogmatic and a workaholic. Additionally, the senior supervisor is intimidated to the point we never meet in the office without another officer present.

As a sworn special police officer, I enforce code and zoning regulations. Unlike law enforcement officers who enforce statutory law and must secure a search warrant to enter private property, in our municipality, if you can see the violation from the public property, you can go on the property to verify what you observe. In most cases, we will request permission from the owner or renter before entering the property. My attention to detail skills resulted in an additional duty with the Environmental Crimes Task Force.

Often, we will coordinate our efforts with the police department when there is a high probability that a criminal enterprise is ongoing. And, on occasion, the situation can go from benign to deadly in a heartbeat.

Following 9-11, due to my previous experience in the terrorist arena, I am tapped to join the municipality's Anti-Terrorism Task Force.

I can go on about the snake I removed from a car, the dog I released from a link-chain collar that was crying out in an abandoned apartment, the woman and her child held against their will in a house secured by barbed wire on all the windows and padlocks affixed to doors on the outside.

My relationship with my senior supervisor turned toxic when I failed to appear as directed at a general call-out following a hurricane; I was remanded to the next senior deputy director for disciplinary action. What surfaced and was ignored by my senior supervisors is that several days prior, I was injured on the job (the unstable side of a structure fell on me) and remained on "no duty" for three additional days. And although no further action is indicated, it was apparent my supervisor wasn't happy with the outcome to the point when I was nominated for and awarded **"Enforcement Officer of the Year,"** my supervisor refused to make the presentation at the awards banquet, leaving that honor to my field supervisor.

###

In most instances, rather than use the few resources available, I either escaped the effects of poor leadership by resigning or was let go. Neither solution mitigates my ongoing struggle with PTSD. And in retrospect, there are specific times when I put myself needlessly in harm's way.

Go-NO Go

So, how can I assess if the situation is such that I am needlessly putting myself, others, or the outcome of a sporting event at risk by taking action without proper backup, or assessing my competency to perform at the highest level?

I returned to my training as a designated Marine Aerial Observer to answer that question.

My responsibilities included familiarizing myself with several aircraft. Our primary aircraft is the OV-10 Bronco. The Bronco's missions included observation, forward air control, helicopter escort, armed reconnaissance, gunfire spotting, utility, and limited attack. The Huey helo, USMC UH-1Ns, was initially introduced in the late 1960s in Vietnam, providing reconnaissance, communications, and close air support to ground forces. When push came to shove, I could find myself aboard any aircraft.

You can appreciate the numerous preflight checks required before taking off on a mission. Aside from a visual check of the aircraft and associated systems, a personal evaluation of my physical and psychological frame of mind is critical. I remember a listing of circumstances that had a numerical value assigned. As you read over the list and check any that applied, if the total is higher than 100, you were down until at least the next day.

Here is a list and the numerical value of each.

1. Late for work, a scheduled briefing, or class: 25
2. Traffic ticket: 25
3. Family birthday, anniversary, special event: 25
4. Medical procedure (physical, dental, etc.): 50
5. Court Appearance: 50
6. Purchase a car: 50
7. Purchase/sell a house: 50
8. Engagement: 50
9. Traffic Accident: 100
10. Failure to make promotions: 100
11. Wedding: 100
12. Serious injury/medical procedure to immediate family member: 100
13. Serious argument with the spouse: 100
14. Death of an immediate family member/co-worker/teammate: 100

The list is not all-inclusive, but you get the picture.

And this listing isn't only applicable to pilots. It can be valuable to any profession that has the possibility of putting the individual or others in harm's way, or the proper outcome of any sporting event in jeopardy. Although the military, law enforcement, fire, and first responders immediately come to mind, also consider medical personnel about to conduct a surgical procedure or emotional trauma counseling. In my role as a soccer official at the highest competitive level, my decision to go forward with an assignment was nearly a disaster.

###

Growing up in Chicago and having many friends in both the PD and the FD, I follow their current situation and the impact suicide has on the force. In mid-July 2020, two police officers and a deputy Commander committed suicide just months apart. So, what might be at the root of similar tragedies?

There are several expansive papers on suicide among military, law enforcement, and first responders.

One is a 2018 study by the **Ruderman Family Foundation**, a philanthropic organization whose mission is to end the stigma associated with mental health. The study found several factors that prevent First Responders from assessing mental health services, including "shame and stigma."

"The same barriers prevent families from talking openly about the suicide of a loved one, thereby contributing to silence and lack of awareness around the issue of first responder suicide."

When co-workers or families do speak up, the possible circumstance that may lead to an officer committing suicide by PERP can surface.

During a recent eulogy for one deceased officer, his wife reveals the newly married couple had their first real fight that morning, and the officer stormed out of the house. Is there a possibility he wasn't in the best frame of mind when he and his partner encountered the shooter?

###

If you are on the outside looking in, you could point to my observations being attributed to paranoia, or poor judgment. Yet, the sheer magnitude of combat or TBI-related incidents in my military and civilian sector careers should have been flagged earlier rather than later. First, I accept my reluctance to highlight my growing inability to face the reality that something is seriously wrong. And secondly, often, the military and corporate leadership weren't prepared or educated to recognize the obvious indicators that something wasn't right in my day-to-day duties or carry out an assignment.

Of course, it's possible my interludes of irrational thoughts or actions were likely submerged sufficiently to not be that obvious to the casual observer. Still, I should have been self-aware enough of how my fixation on mission "at all costs", was likely to result in damage to more than my ego.

I am in the backyard cutting the lawn as the phone rings off the hook, and I wonder why no one is picking it up. Duh. Everyone else is out. The kids are at school, and my wife is at the doctor's office. And I'm the only one at home. I could let it go to voicemail, but something tells me it's important. Taking off my gloves, I pick up the receiver, "Hello?"

"Arn, Bud Williams here; I'm glad I've got you. I have some great news." Bud is the commissioner of assignments for college soccer officials. "You've been put forward as the center official for the college semi-finals on November 3rd. Are you available?"

Am I available? Of course, I'm available.

Bud says that only two officials were considered, and I was the first choice.

We continued exchanging pleasantries, and I told Bud I was grateful for his confidence in me. He continues that he has every reason to believe I'll do a great job.

As I hang up, I hear my wife drive up to the house. I am so pumped and excited to tell her the good news.

My wife gets out of the car slowly, and I reach over to help her. She looks to be in great pain. In answer to my unasked question, she tells me that the pain she's been having isn't just a stomach ache; it's a cyst on her intestinal lining, and she will need minor surgery to remove it. The doctor made an appointment at Portsmouth Naval Hospital for November 3rd.

November 3rd. That's the same date as my assignment for the soccer match. What am I going to do?

My wife settled comfortably in the den; I got her some water, and, in answer to her question on how my day has gone, I told her of Bud's call and my assignment. Immediately, and so like her, she congratulated me and said how proud of me she was.

When I tell her the date, she ponders it a second, saying she doesn't see a problem. Her ninety-minute surgery is scheduled for 0730, and my match is at 1600, less than thirty minutes from the hospital. All appears good to go.

The morning of the surgery, we are up at 0500, and the car is packed. My wife has sufficient clothing and such in her bag, and I have all my referee uniforms and equipment in the trunk.

My wife is prepped for the surgery and enters the OR precisely at 0730. Sitting in the waiting room, I take out the team rundown for today's match and begin mental prep.

Looking at the wall clock, I see the time is nearly 0930, and the surgery is projected to take less than ninety minutes. At 1100, the surgeon exits the OR and, coming in my direction, sits down.

Lieutenant Colonel, your wife is out of surgery but is in serious condition. She has ovarian cancer. At worst, she has two months to two years to live.

I fight the urge to slump back into my seat. I ask if there is nothing that can be done. The doctor relates that there is an experimental protocol involving Taxol, a chemotherapy drug, and he is sure he can get her approved to begin. He goes on that she is heavily sedated and won't be able to be seen until much later tonight, around 2000.

Doing some quick math, I rationalize I can still do the match, and even should it go into overtime, I can easily be back at the hospital when my wife wakes up. I thank the doctor, go to the parking garage, and drive to the soccer complex across town. I'm very early, but I need time to think.

The standing procedure is for the officiating team to arrive at the complex ninety minutes before kick-off. Giving the officials sufficient time to review the pregame planning, inspect the teams, and walk the pitch.

Although I am doing my best to maintain an in-control, positive front, one of the officials and a long-time friend asks if I'm OK. He believes something is on my mind. It isn't a big deal, I say. Fifteen minutes before kick-off, we enter the complex.

To an outside observer, everything is going as it should. The match started precisely on time, play was moving well, and both teams were aggressive but well under control. Ten minutes into the match, on one challenge, the home team gets past the defenders and beats the keeper for a goal. The home crowd goes wild, and all appears good.

Establishing eye contact with my assistant referees, I whistle for the restart. Physically, I was keeping up with play, but mentally, I was beginning to lose focus. At about the twenty-minute mark, it finally hits me. My wife is lying in the hospital and slowly dying. What am I doing here?

In front of nearly one thousand fans in the stands, I fall to one knee and, as quietly as possible, start to cry. The spectators in the stands quiet as my assistant referee and the home team coach (a friend of many years) ask if I am OK.

The match is delayed for about five minutes to give me a chance to get my act together, and I finish the match. In the final assessment, the home team won decisively and without any controversial decisions on my part or that of the officiating crew.

To begin with, I should have never accepted the assignment in the first place once I knew my wife was going into surgery the same day. Upon notification of the severity of her situation, I should have immediately called the commissioner and informed him of the problem. He would have recognized the serious nature of my reluctance to do the game and likely appreciated my honesty.

That is solid leadership. We should always keep in mind that the real mission isn't carrying out the assigned schedule, but recognition that schedules can be changed. This is an example of a non-life-threatening situation. At worst, an improper decision on my part may have led to the wrong team winning, and the fans disappointed.

Yet, when it comes to a similar bad decision by an individual, or leadership among professions with inherent dangerous situations, serious injury, or death may result, with the outcome likely to be worse than a few folks being disappointed.

Here's the rub. Just walk down the corridors of any VAMC, and you will see veterans missing limbs, an eye(s), and or sitting quietly waiting for treatment. In addition, many suffer from TBIs, and the number of combat-related PTSDs continues to grow. Is it any wonder that if leadership is lacking at the highest levels, the casualties only increase at the lower?

In a *Lexipol* study by **Karen Lansing** in 2006, Marines, Army, and National Guard forces activated downrange were assessed.

Within the Marines, teams operating in consistently high levels of combat engagement and rated their leaders as "high" in positive leadership skills had a 19 percent incidence of psychological hardship (e.g., PTSD, depression, anxiety). For those who rated their leaders as "low" in positive leadership skills, the incidence of psychological hardship rose to 44 percent.

Lancing continues:

"That's a staggering spread," she said, "but it reflects the largest obstacle I encounter in my work. *"The biggest problem I have when treating duty-induced PTSD isn't with neutralizing the event and facilitating the opportunity for adaptive learning for the first responder. I can take care of that very easily. But if I encounter trauma after the event rendered due to poor leadership, I may never be able to bring their officer back."*

###

Lastly, remember, this isn't just about PTSD and suicide in general; it's about how I am fighting active suicidal ideation and winning. And while some folks might be offended by my recollections, I suggest they look closely into their situation and assess if they are the victim or the contributor to a suicide resulting from their inaction or direction.

Chapter 6
You Can't Save Everyone

Sometimes I reflect on the training I've provided, especially the safety-related, and I remember a saying a good friend passed on to me:

It's OK to Look Back...But Don't Stare!

On its surface, it may appear straightforward. Yet, this warning is like someone telling you not to think about Mickey Mouse. Sure enough, an image of Mickey Mouse continues to pop up for the remainder of the day. I can say the same thing about training-related memories that replay in loop fashion when I dream or embarrassingly teach a class.

For example:

I've been a sailing instructor trainer for over a quarter-century. If you've been in my class, you know that **"Arn's Rule #1"** - you will always wear a personal flotation device (PFD) anytime you work on or near the water. Now there are times when my staff or someone I'm working with will not wear their PFD correctly, and I can get upset about that to the point where I fired my best instructor on one specific occasion. Some folks might think that was harsh.

But I look at it in two ways.

1. If I can't trust you to carry out my most important rule, what else will you do when I am not in the area?
2. If you are an instructor, you lead by example. The students look to you for instruction, motivation, and an example of the kind of sailor they want to be when they grow up. So when one of your students sees you

not wearing your PFD, they may think it's okay for them not to wear theirs or ignore other rules.

Another example is one of my students in a disabled sailing program who spent most of the summer with me. On the last day of sailing, he told me he was returning to his club upstate and thought I needed to know that he wouldn't wear the PFD. He thought my rule number one didn't pertain to him. Several weeks later, I received a call from a good friend who told me this sailor had fallen out of his boat and drowned in a terrible accident.

###

Since retiring from the Marine Corps, I've had a few exciting career moves; one was working for an organization that primarily trained law enforcement, first responders, and, on occasion, military personnel. While still on active duty in the military in my last eleven years, my background was primarily working in joint commands specializing in terrorism-related issues. In addition, I had an opportunity to work with host nation special operations forces worldwide. Consequently, I gained a lot of experience getting inside the heads of terrorists, how they operated, and how they thought. And how to best keep from falling victim to a terrorist operation.

Following 9/11, while working with a municipality environmental crimes task force, I found that my expertise in the anti-terrorism world was again a sought-after commodity, thus making several presentations to first responders, police, and fire throughout the region. As a result, I was offered a position with a company that trained law enforcement on various immediate response scenarios. During my time with that organization, I worked with U.S. Coast Guard personnel trained as a forerunner of the Deployable Operations Group (DOG) and, later, the Maritime Security Response Team (MSRT). In this case, these individuals were about to deploy to the Persian Gulf.

Real-world Examples Military

As part of the training, I provided examples of how terrorists operate on land and water. One was an Israeli security craft responding to an unauthorized fishing vessel close to an oil rig in the Mediterranean Sea. I explained that as the Israeli vessel closed with the unauthorized boat, they observed two fishermen with poles in the water. Approaching within hailing distance, the Israelis informed the two fishermen that they had to leave the area immediately. Receiving no response from the fishermen, the fishing boat exploded as the Israelis closed in, injuring numerous crew on the Israeli security vessel.

Near the end of April 2004, the U.S. Naval vessel in the northern Persian Gulf with U.S. Coast Guard personnel aboard approached a similar fishing craft near a restricted area. Again, hailing the fishing vessel and receiving no response, the U.S. Navy security vessel closed to the fishing vessel. It exploded, injuring several and killing two U.S. Naval personnel and one U.S. Coast Guardsman. It's possible that the Coast Guardsman killed was in my class.

###

Training Exercises Military

I worked with boarding party personnel in another Coast Guard training exercise. The scenario is this: intelligence identified a fishing vessel in the Caribbean transporting explosives from Colombia toward New Orleans, Louisiana. The information indicates there are two terrorists on board. The standard crew for this vessel is six fishermen plus the captain, for a total of seven. The U.S. Coast Guard cutter vectored into the vessel's location, and from a standoff position, the boarding officer hails the fishing vessel and orders it to go dead in the water. Now, I turn the exercise over to one of the boarding officers in the class.

The boarding officer orders the ship's crew to the vessel's stern, and the captain remains in the wheelhouse. The total visible is seven individuals. After a time and no additional crew visible, the boarding officer decides to close in and board the vessel. Unfortunately, when the cutter was close to the fishing vessel, the terrorist below deck caused the explosion.

In the debrief, I asked the boarding officer what he would have done if the fishing vessel hadn't exploded. And he said he would have put a boarding party aboard. So my suggestion was that without any credible information that there were no terrorists aboard, I would have ordered the captain and crew to the vessel's stern, 3 had them enter their safety boats, and left the vicinity of the larger fishing vessel. Then I would have sunk the fishing vessel.

This may not be a standard operating procedure, but terrorists aren't concerned with SOP.

I have crafted numerous training scenarios focused on a possible terrorist threat to an established U.S. military facility or civilian maritime infrastructure during my active duty and civilian life. For example, in one scenario, I successfully closed off egress from the southern Hampton Roads cities of Norfolk and Virginia Beach.

Law Enforcement

Another terrorist-related or active shooter exercise I directed is a no-notice SWATEX that included SWAT personnel from seven regional municipalities, State Police, FBI, and CIA.

Still, another focuses on a law enforcement response to a similar situation following the tragic Virginia Tech campus shooting. An active shooter or shooters attack the church, killing and injuring several and taking four hostages into the surrounding mountain range. Once again, several municipalities' police, fire, and additional first responders had to locate and identify the terrorists and hostages, work out a plan, effectively secure the immediate area end using State Police assets and successfully gain their release and capture the terrorists.

Defense Against School Shootings

Even in retirement, my unique skills can help the community. For example, following the Sandy Hook School shootings, I approached my grandchildren's school and offered a security survey. On the surface, I was pleased to observe the school uses single access, a personnel security badge, and a floor monitor system. Diving deeper, I locate, at the back door, a key for the door under a potted plant, allowing teachers and coaches access rather than using the front door. The school grounds are beautiful but open to the public. A large stand of trees stretching several hundred yards from the school is in the rear playground. Teachers congregate at a table near the school building and nearly one hundred yards from an area close to the trees where most students play. I worked my way to just inside the tree line. As the children passed by my location, I played the part of a groundskeeper, and I told the kids I cut my hand on a saw and asked for help. Two children came into the trees and were close enough for me to grab them. I could have snatched the child and run back to my car in an actual situation. But, in my report to the Head of School and the following presentation to key staff, I was surprised when one teacher said they sat at that table because it provided shade. No show of concern for the students was evident, except it was an inconvenience to them. The attitude that it can't happen here remains alive and well.

Soccer

In a speech by **Winston Churchill** in 1906, he was quoted as saying: ***"Where there is great power, there is great responsibility,"***

Early on, I mentioned that I would threaten to "rip someone's lips off" if they couldn't get the point I was trying to impress on them. And in my position as first a Marine NCO and later a commissioned officer, I've witnessed the results of those individuals not following my directions. In combat, the impact of their actions and, or my orders, can cause the loss of life.

It's sometimes challenging to rationalize that I am not responsible for their deaths, but I still profoundly feel that loss.

Still, that's in a combat scenario, but what about when it involves playing a game?

In my nearly three decades as a National Assessor with the US Soccer Federation, I am responsible for evaluating the referee's performance and officiating team members, often at the sport's highest level. In the USA, this is Major League Soccer. It takes work for an official to rise to this level, and my decision can lead to their advancement or relegation to a lower ranking.

At this stage in my career, I didn't fully realize the true impact I was having on them as individuals. I also didn't have the training to assess the signs and symptoms of their mental health. When an official's poor performance could be attributed to a temporary loss of focus or misapplication of the Laws of the Game, I was missing the subtle indications that the official was already in trouble before the whistle blew for the match's start.

I'm sure that sports officials and players have personal rituals they perform before a big game. My favorite was watching tapes of referee performances at the game's highest level the night before. I've witnessed others walking the empty stadium, throwing up, laying out their uniform in a particular manner and sequence.

Although I can attend the referee's pregame briefing, some referees prefer I not be present. Immediately following the match, and the official's performance could be better, I've been asked not to conduct the assessment but instead do it later by conference call or email. A clear indicator the referee is signaling relief at a good performance is when they reach for a bottle of their favorite libation.

If my assessment is pivotal to the advancement of the referee, a review by the powers can be instantaneous. Especially where the expected outcome results in the official attaining placement on the much-coveted International Referee List.

This is the system's upside, but what happens when the official's performance needs to be better and results in non-advancement or relegation to a lower level?

I know of several officials at the highest level of the game and among referees striving for the top to attempt or successfully commit suicide. Had I been better trained to recognize the signs or deliver my assessment more positively, could this have been avoided?

"These examples are little more than sad stories to the general public. Yet, each time I failed to prevent the loss of life, it made my will to live difficult."

I don't want to give you the impression that everything I did has a sad ending.

During a Boy Scout Camporee, and on the last day, a scoutmaster entered the headquarters carrying a scout in his arms. The scout, to rid his tent of mosquitos, liberally sprayed insect repellent and went back to sleep. The combination of an unvented tent and spray became toxic. Putting my First Aid skills to work, I checked for responsiveness and detected none, had another leader call 911, and started CPR. I continued until relieved by EMS personnel. The scout recovered in the ambulance en route to the hospital. For my quick actions, **I was awarded my second N-MCAM for lifesaving and recognized as the City of Tampa Bay runner-up as Military Citizen of the Year.**

In 1985, as part of our security evaluations in Pakistan, I suggested to the Colonel that we go up to the hill town of Murree. During my assignment to the American Embassy in the late 1960s, I often traveled to Murree and, at one time, considered retiring there. Now Murree isn't just a beautiful little town in the mountains of Pakistan. It contains the summer lodges of many embassies, and some were constructed initially during the British Raj period of the mid-nineteenth century. Temperatures can get well over 100° near the capital city of Islamabad, so Murree is the ideal location to escape the heat. In addition to the lodges is the Murree Christian School. The majority of the students come from diplomatic communities and government officials. After traveling a long, winding, steep, and dangerous road, we arrived at Murree, and I showed our team around and pointed out the significant Pakistani military presence. Once we arrived at the school and I introduced the director to our team and explained our mission in the country, we were permitted to walk the grounds. Unfortunately, the school needed to have what I considered proper security. The school is mainly open to the public, and its security is no more than crowd control. Therefore, we recommended a security wall surrounding the compound and arm security at the entrance. I had no idea if the school would raise the money to implement security measures. Fast forward to 2002, possibly, to show non-support for Pakistan president Musharraf coming in on the side of the United States during the war on terror in Afghanistan, an attack is conducted on Murree Christian School. The estimated three masked men burst into Murree Christian School, killing two security guards, a cook, a carpenter, a receptionist, and another person. Miraculously, none of the 146 missionary students are injured. In response, Murree Christian School moved temporarily to Thailand. Fortunately, sometimes folks listen.

###

In a speech by **Winston Churchill** in 1906, he was quoted as saying: ***"Where there is great power, there is great responsibility,"***

Early on, I mentioned that I would threaten to "rip someone's lips off" if they couldn't get the point I was trying to impress on them. And in my position as first a Marine NCO and later a commissioned officer, I've witnessed the results of those individuals not following my directions. In combat, the impact of their actions and, or my orders, can cause the loss of life. It's sometimes challenging to rationalize that I am not responsible for their deaths, but I still profoundly feel that loss.

Still, that's in a combat scenario, but what about when it involves playing a game?

In my nearly three decades as a National Assessor with the US Soccer Federation, I am responsible for evaluating the referee's performance and officiating team members, often at the sport's highest level. In the USA, this is Major League Soccer. It takes work for an official to rise to this level, and my decision can lead to their advancement or relegation to a lower ranking.

At this stage in my career, I didn't fully realize the true impact I was having on them as individuals. I also didn't have the training to assess the signs and symptoms of their mental health. When an official's poor performance could be attributed to a temporary loss of focus or misapplication of the Laws of the Game, I was missing the subtle indications that the official was already in trouble before the whistle blew for the match's start.

I'm sure that sports officials and players have personal rituals they perform before a big game. My favorite was watching tapes of referee performances at the game's highest level the night before. I've witnessed others walking the empty stadium, throwing up, and laying out their uniforms in a particular manner and sequence. Although I can attend the referee's pregame briefing, some referees prefer I not be present. Immediately following the match, and the official's performance could be better, I've been asked not to conduct the assessment but instead do it later by conference call or email.

A clear indicator the referee is signaling relief at a good performance is when they reach for a bottle of their favorite libation.

If my assessment is pivotal to the advancement of the referee, a review by the powers can be instantaneous. Especially where the expected outcome results in the official attaining placement on the much-coveted International Referee List.

This is the system's upside, but what happens when the official's performance needs to be better and results in non-advancement or relegation to a lower level?

I know of several officials at the highest level of the game and among referees striving for the top to attempt or successfully commit suicide. Had I been better trained to recognize the signs or deliver my assessment more positively, could this have been avoided?

I continued to see my former wife frequently and often had supper with her and Jim, and for a period of time following a seriously debilitating illness, I lived in their house. We were truly the odd threesome. Jim's focus remained on his job, with little observable true love and affection for my wife. As her cancer progressed, she and I would sit on their back lanai and recount our day. Compared to hers mine is mundane. To be completely honest, I just wanted to be close to her. To lessen the impact of her chemotherapy-induced peripheral neuropathy and relieve lymphedema, a massage therapist visits the house several times weekly. Over time I realized Jim was returning home earlier than usual and often when the therapist was about to leave. This fact is not lost on my former wife. Within months of her passing, Jim marries the therapist.

Jim's action so soon felt like a betrayal, and possibly to assuage my feelings, I may have sought opportunities to push common sense limits when doing my job. In this case, it's the operation of a chop shop.

My mission today is to go to the rear of the residential property, where a three-car garage is located. If I can hear the sound of activity such as drills, saws, or other machinery, I will approach the structure, knock on the door, identify myself as zoning enforcement, and enter.

Here's how it fell out.

Armed with a badge, radio, and an overabundance of hubris, I enter the building. Inside revealed at least six men disassembling several cars. I begin to talk quickly. "So, how's it going, fellas? Oh, you guys must be a Honda and Nissan car club.

Glancing down, I saw a VIN plate on the ground. By this time, the men in the garage were thankfully struck dumb by my actions. Picking up the VIN plate, I said, "Hey guys, you can't be taking cars apart like this in a residential neighborhood." And I turned and walked out the door and down the driveway—total time in the garage less than one minute. Although, in retrospect, it felt like a lifetime.

High Noon in the City

My assignment to a high-crime area of the city wasn't without low spots.

In my duties, I attend neighborhood civic meetings informing concerned citizens (read: busy-bodies and grandmas) of our activities in the area. I enjoyed these meetings because I could meet face-to-face with folks over cookies and diet soda. A chorus of "Amens and Praise God" punctuated my remarks if a particular topic hit home. In a genuine show of solidarity, I'd often end my comments with, "Have a Blessed day!"

On one occasion, as I walked through a troubled neighborhood, an elderly woman sitting on her porch called out, "Aren't you the officer from the other day?" Nodding my head in agreement, she asked me to come up and chat.

After exchanging pleasantries and commenting, she believed I was a "God-fearing man" and asked if I would pray with her. Although she remained seated in her rocking chair, I knelt and bowed my head. "Dear Lord," she began in a loud voice. And, in a quieter voice, she whispered to me that the young men standing on the corner were waiting for me because I impounded a car for abandonment and harassed a man for releasing untreated sewage (the man dumped over 5,000 gallons from a tanker truck into the storm drain directly into the river).

A reasonable man would take the hint and depart. But then, I always had more guts than common sense in those days.

Walking straight toward the lads, I asked, "Which of you abandoned the car in the street that I towed away?" Initially, they remained silent. Then one said it was his car. Turning toward him, I asked if he would walk me to where the vehicle was towed less than fifty yards from our location. Agreeing, I asked him if he knew the transmission fluid was leaking into the street as he and I walked. After he acknowledged he did, which was why he left it in the street, I mentioned that since the vehicle remains registered in his name, he is responsible for it. Working or not. To get the car from the impound lot will cost about one hundred dollars. The fine for knowingly discharging oil or a hazardous substance into a storm drain could be three years and $5,000 - 50,000 per day. Once that sunk in, he turned to me, held his hand, and thanked me. To rub a bit of oil into the wound, I told him I couldn't write it up without evidence of a spill. A week later, after praying with grandma, I walked toward the spill, and the area was scrubbed clean.

Chapter 7
Suicidal Behavior and the Role of Religion and Spirituality

The subject of religion can be a turn-off for the secular side of society, but I have found that, as the Eric Davis quote goes:

If you don't believe in something, you'll fall for anything.

Also, I have a different spin on that:

If you only believe in yourself, you'll often be disappointed.

Note that although disappointment can cause anxiety, that's part of life. But if you have no one to turn to in your time of need other than yourself, expect to fall short of your expectations, especially if they are unrealistic.

As we travel through life, we gather some folks around us who become sources of inspiration, consolation, and some a source of desolation.

My mom is an excellent source of prophetic sayings:

- ➤ Drink too much water before bed; you must get up at night.
- ➤ That girl is common. She may appear to be a great catch. Beware of what you catch.
- ➤ Taking your new radio to the park will only get it stolen. It was!
- ➤ This paddling will hurt me more than it will you.
- ➤ You must put your name on your camp clothes to keep them. I returned from camp with only a wet swimsuit.

> ➢ And when I left for Vietnam. Make sure you come back with every body part you went with.

As a rule, I never really had what I would call a "best friend." I have many acquaintances but few genuine friends and no best friends. Eddie proved the exception and is the basis for my rule.

A truly best friend is always there when needed and likely is there without being asked. They are always in your corner and clear-minded enough to tell you the truth when it's time to throw in the towel.

On the other hand, an acquaintance, roommate, teammate, or classmate can come and go, remain in the back of your mind, and be a source of minor emotional disturbance should injury or misfortune befall them.

The one constant with acquaintances is they often look at life through a prism of their own making. And any counsel they offer may not be in your best interest.

So, I've turned to strengthen my belief in God. God asks that I believe in His perfect love for me. He never demands more from me than what I may be capable of at the time and continually encourages me to improve on my weaknesses. As with my mom, as I fall short or disappoint often, I know He will always welcome me back.

You might say that this is all good, but does a belief in something greater than oneself make a difference in someone considering suicide or surviving a suicide attempt?

If you can believe you are not the end-all and be-all, then believing in a Creator who imbues each of us with a soul

90

opens up a whole panoply of possibilities that make life worth living.

As a catechist, my belief in the Creator is amply revealed through the Catholic RCIA, Confirmation, and theology programs and the Catechism of the Catholic Church's outline using the traditional four pillars of Catholic catechisms: faith, liturgy/sacraments, life in Christ, and prayer, which Peter distills in Acts 2:42.

For me, this is sufficient, though when speaking to my students, especially those coming with biases or near disbelief, I supplement class with lessons from the Seven Essentials modules material of **Credible Catholic**, a Magis Center curriculum correlated to the Catechism of the Catholic Church. © Magis Center 2017 2 The founder and president of the Magis Center, **Fr. Robert Spitzer, S.J., PH.D.** is also the former president of Gonzaga University.

I met Fr. Spitzer when he was the **In the Defense of the Faith** presenter at the Order of Malta Federal Association Investiture weekend held in 2018.

In Credible Catholic, Presentation 1, CHAPTER 1, **Proof of a Soul and Heaven from Near-Death Experiences (NDEs)**, there are five NDE studies from medical professionals and scientists that highlight their observations of their patients, each of which is eye-opening and cause for the belief we do have a transcendent soul. I am particularly interested in the interview by Dr. Raymond Moody with Dr. Bruce Greyson, then of the University of Virginia. Dr. Greyson has been studying NDEs for over 30 years. He has been called the "Father of Near-Death Experience Research."

Dr. Greyson described the change he noticed in many of his patients as a result of their NDEs, saying:

- "They lose their fear of living life to the fullest because they are not afraid of taking chances anymore. They're not afraid of dying. So, they get more interested in life and enjoy it much more than they did before."

In answer to a question by Dr. Moody as to if people that made suicide attempts and had an NDE as a result, "When they recover do they have a desire to commit suicide?" Dr. Greyson answers,

- "They do not! Patients are saying they no longer are considering suicide as an option. Usually, because they see their problem in a different perspective, they no longer identify with this bag of skin. They think of something greater than themselves. Their problems are not enough to end this life."

My major takeaway is that when an individual survives a suicide attempt and experiences an NDE, there is a strong belief that there is more to life than just the present. And knowing this, they are no longer under the misconception that the only answer to a problem is suicide.

The Power of Prayer

I believe that God's Word and Commandments are the cornerstones for His Church and all, believers and not, to live according to natural law. And that the United States looks to its Judeo-Christian roots for faith, wisdom, and inspiration.

The Jewish first verse of the Shema relates to the kingship of God. The verse, "Hear, O Israel: the LORD our God is One LORD," is clear. We cannot worship a panoply of gods, be they deities or personal demons of greed, gluttony, or sloth.

I am a firm believer that prayer works. Sometimes it's a conversation with God, a request for Mary to intercede, or a specific saint to give me strength by their example to overcome a failure or refocus on what is essential.

Recently, I went to Confession with a visiting priest in my parish. I related to Father that I am writing a book on suicide. As I reviewed the stories of folks I knew who have first-hand experience with the suicide of a family member, close friend, or even an attempt themselves, I found myself spiraling deeper into a very dark place. Was this an indication I should stop writing? If not, how can I find the strength to move forward without damaging myself?

Minutes passed before Father offered that, at times such as I highlighted, we need to seek the assistance of a saint known to strengthen those suffering in a specific way. His suggestion is Saint Dymphna, the Patron Saint for the Mentally Ill. She lived in 7th-century Ireland and was martyred by her father, an Irish king. When the king's wife died, he was so distraught he sought to marry Dymphna because she closely resembled the queen. Dymphna escaped to Belgium. Once her father received information about Dymphna's location, he traveled there and made his desires known. She again refused, and he cut off her head.

I was looking for help from Father, but I was substituting my lousy situation for another. Accepting my penance, I exit the confessional. On my knees, I pray to Saint Dymphna and ask for her assistance. Within days my mind began to clear. And, more importantly, when a thought surfaces that had in the past caused mental distress when I call upon Saint Dymphna, I am back in a good place.

I am in contact with many close friends asking themselves, "What can I do to help before it's too late?" This prayer to Saint Dymphna succinctly identifies her as the well-known patron saint of those with mental or nervous disorders or mental illness.

Good Saint Dymphna, great wonder-worker in every affliction of mind and body, I humbly implore your powerful intercession with Jesus through Mary, the Health of the Sick, in my present need. (Mention it.) Saint Dymphna, the martyr of purity, patroness of those who suffer from nervous and mental afflictions, beloved child of Jesus and Mary, pray to Them for me and obtain my request. (Pray one Our Father, one Hail Mary and one Glory Be.) Saint Dymphna, Virgin and Martyr, pray for us.

The Prayer to Saint Dymphna is just one off-ramp that can be taken leading away from the active or passive suicidal ideation highway. Please share this with anyone who fits my introduction. And, for those that may not believe in God, I offer you Pascal's Wager. What have you got to lose?

Pascal's Wager argues that as humans bet on God's existence with the fates of their eternities, the rational person ought to believe and live as if God exists. If they analyze the payoffs of believing and disbelieving in God, one ought to believe in God to avoid eternal damnation and in the hope of achieving eternal life.

###

In combat, prayer is often silent. However, prayer becomes an acclimation spoken aloud to give strength to win through a particularly tough situation. I remember the story of an individual that should have died due to multiple severe injuries (arm ripped off at the shoulder, chest, and leg crushed). Instead, when finally extracted from the vehicle, the corpsman looked up, amazed that the casualty was still talking. By leaning closer, he heard, "Hail Mary full of Grace...". The casualty was praying the Rosary held firmly in the hand of the remaining arm. He did survive. Since that day, I have carried my Rosary everywhere.

###

I am seated next to a Captain in the Air Force at a formal dinner. He's a flight surgeon and leads a tactical evacuation care (TEC) team. This team has personnel and equipment aboard their aircraft to provide immediate trauma care.

Knowing I am a Marine, the Captain tells me of a recent event involving a female Marine Lance Corporal (E-3). His team, based in Germany, regularly deployed aboard a C-17. The pre-briefing of the team takes place as the aircraft wings its way from Germany to Iraq in response to a request by the Marine General commanding. The L/Cpl suffers from sepsis, an extreme reaction to an infection that causes inflammatory chemicals to be released into the bloodstream.

Once the casualty is aboard, and during the five-hour flight, the team fights what most medical professionals consider a losing battle. They stabilized her at least four times. Upon arrival in Germany, the top medical officer pronounces nothing to do except keep her as comfortable as possible.

Not willing to give up, the Captain resorts to a "Hail Mary play"...literally. He calls back to the states to members of Our Order, who immediately begin a prayer circle asking God, the Divine Physician, to intervene. Within an hour, the L/Cpl starts moving in the bed. Thirty minutes later, she is speaking coherently. Five hours after the medical professionals wrote her off, she ate and talked with her mom back in the States. Divine intervention?

###

I recently listened to Ascension's *Catechism in a Year* podcast with Father Mike Schmitz, Day 111. I enjoy these podcasts because they increase my understanding of the Church and often leave me with a nugget of gold that helps me through the day. So, here's my nugget for the day. NO! For life:

"... there's an incredible gift about being part of the body of Christ, but there's also responsibility...when one member suffers, we all suffer when one member is glorified and honored, we all are glorified and honored... among other things it means there's no such thing as a private sin there's no such thing as private virtue either... it hurts me and hurts all those that we love... So it's you're struggling against sin, you struggle for virtue that strengthens me even if I never know about it...one of the things it reminds us is especially if you find yourself isolated and alone and say, well because I'm isolated and alone my life doesn't matter...the church steps in right now and says that is absolutely incorrect that is absolutely backward ...when you're battling you know striving for the Lord. You feel like, man; I'm just slogging away, and for what? Well, thank you so much for each other when you are strengthened, it strengthens the rest of us...when you fight, you're fighting for us...when you pray, you're praying for all of us."

Knowing that I am part of the Body of Christ, and many are sharing in my struggles, not in a sympathetic way, but in a strengthening team effort, gives me the confidence to press on no matter the obstacle or self-doubt. I am praying for you; please pray for me. Today. Tomorrow. Until we meet in God's heavenly arms with love.

###

In 2003, St. Pope John Paul II addressed the theme of depression. His remarks can be applied to all those who struggle with mental illness, their loved ones, and those who care for them. He noted that depression "is always a spiritual trial." By saying this, he did not deny that mental illness has biological or psychological causes, which it surely does; rather, he recognized that mental illness also impacts our spiritual life in unique ways: "This disease is often accompanied by an existential and spiritual crisis that leads to an inability to perceive the meaning of life."

###

While the Church teaches that suicide is contrary to the will of God who gave us life, at the same time, the Church recognizes that "grave psychological disturbances, anguish, or grave fear of hardship, suffering, or torture can diminish the responsibility of the one committing suicide." The Catechism of the Catholic Church instructs us that "We should not despair of the eternal salvation of persons who have taken their own lives. By ways known to him alone, God can provide the opportunity for salutary repentance. The Church prays for persons who have taken their own lives."

###

I mentioned earlier that it's critically important that I remain busy, and a quick scan of my calendar contained in Chapter 10 will support that premise. You may even think I need more time to take on one more project. Yet here I go again.

I've come to accept that the issue of mental health is pervasive throughout society; it's entrenched. In the workplace, schools, in our homes, and the pews. So, I started doing what I do best, researching where I can get help should a mental health crisis surface in Church. I'm certified in CPR and know where the AED is located in the commons, so if a parishioner should be suffering a heart attack, I'm confident I could render immediate first aid and possibly save a life. But what if someone presents the symptoms of a mental health challenge?

According to Johns Hopkins Medicine, "An estimated 26% of Americans ages 18 and older -- about 1 in 4 adults -- suffers from a diagnosable mental disorder in a given year. Many people suffer from more than one mental disorder at a given time. In particular, depressive illnesses co-occur with substance use and anxiety disorders."

Anxiety and stress can manifest visually: a person may appear restless or unable to sit still, complain of headaches, backache or other aches and pains, rapid breathing, sweating, or hot flashes. A more unsettling action may be sudden outbursts or aggressive gestures, especially from a parishioner known to be quiet and reserved. I can see the situation unfold, but am I confident enough to know how I can assist?

My research shows several recognized programs provide the training necessary to assist someone experiencing a mental health challenge. And, as you might expect, it's called **Mental Health-First Aid**.

Mental Health-First Aid is an international program to teach the skills to respond to the signs of mental illness and substance use. This day-long course is taught both in-person and virtually. I took the virtual course and am hooked and confident I can render assistance. Yet, I am only one person.

If I were to ask the congregation to raise their hands if they have received basic first aid and CPR at some point in their lives, a majority would raise their hands. The reality is that nearly sixty-five percent will not be current. I'm sure that following a heart attack at church, if the parish offered CPR training, a significant number would renew their certification.

The response to the offer of scheduling a Mental Health-First Aid course may not be as widely accepted. Heart attacks are considered a normal part of life while responding to a mental health challenge is too many steps too far.

How do I move my passion to help from concept to reality?

I am totally against recreating the wheel. Again, further research surfaces a credible organization supported by Bishops and Pastors across the USA already exists. It's the **Association of Catholic Mental Health Ministers (CMHM)**. With their guidance and resources as the cornerstone, the foundation to build a Mental Health Ministry is in hand. On the micro-scale is establishing a Mental Health Ministry at the parish level. On the macro scale, Diocese wide.

My efforts are still in their infancy, but hopefully, by the time this book is published, the Mental Health Ministry will be well on its way, God willing.

Chapter 8
Research: Personally and Unscientifically Conducted

I'm sure the first word out of my mouth soon after I was born was, "Why?" Why am I still hungry? Why am I still wet? Why am I not the center of your world? And, well into adulthood, "Why?" remains front and center.

In this chapter, I present the professional literature I've researched to guide me away from suicidal ideation; and the results of using myself as the guinea pig to substantiate or refute my findings. In some cases, my goal is to compile data I can present to my primary care physician (PCP) to support my desire not to take a recommended prescription drug.

After three years of following my research and most often in agreement with my PCP and mental health professionals, I am off all prescription drugs except one. At my most recent semi-annual physical, my PCP recommended I take Lisinopril. Previously, I was on hydrochlorothiazide, and Pfizer recalled it because of elevated levels of potential cancer-causing impurities. The compromise is that I participate in a 90-day program monitoring my BP twice daily. The VA provided a BP cuff and Bluetooth CareConsole® Mobile Hub to record and forward data directly to the Telehealth Department at McGuire in real-time.

I was impressed with their conscientious monitoring. Occasionally, my BP was over 165/90, and I immediately received a call to check if I was OK. For the first month, I took my first reading as soon as I woke in the morning and again just before retiring for the evening. After that, my numbers needed to be more consistent, and there was some concern.

Again, because I wanted to know "Why?" I researched how and when to take my BP correctly. It's not that the Telehealth Department didn't provide solid guidance; I, as with many men, didn't read the directions.

I began taking my BP immediately after the prompt, which was uniformly high. I kept a log, and several reasons stood out: my dogs were barking, my daughter sent a text asking if I was OK, I was running late, etc. So, I took it a second time alone, in a quiet location. The result? A drop of twenty to thirty points. And lastly, I took it a third time using my Mindfulness training, and the numbers fell into the 120/the 70s. My conclusion is that when the BP is taken correctly, my numbers will likely remain well within limits, and the necessity of taking any BP meds is negated.

Impact of TBI

"The person with TBI and PTSD is living in a state unlike anything previously experienced. For the family, home is no longer the safe haven but an unfamiliar front with unpredictable and sometimes frightening currents and events."

Writing about how mental and physical trauma impacts my life when as I've mentioned, I've had multiple traumatic events is challenging. The combination of events such as the riots in Pakistan, going into a burning building, and being t-boned in my city car is a new ball game.

Some takeaways:

➤ If I follow my dad's lead, I should always excel but never seek recognition for my successes.

➤ That gives rise to the deep emotional mood I retreat to whenever I am recognized for excellent performance or awarded a military decoration.

➤ Or not trusting my superiors who demonstrate a lack of solid leadership traits putting those under them at unnecessary risk.

➤ Actions that cause me to either "take one for the team" or push the envelope to succeed without endangering others.

In each of the above, I become withdrawn from those I should be most close to, in the workplace, church, or family. I prefer to be the hermit ready to quickly complete a task, thus limiting the possibility of establishing close relationships.

Let's start with the TBIs.

The first I remember is in sixth grade in grammar school. Four years my senior, my cousin walked me to school. On this particular day, his sixteen-year-old friend drives the family car and stops alongside the street we were walking—my cousin steps inside the car. I stand on the back bumper, looking through the window. For an unknown reason, the driver hits the gas, and with no way to hold on, I fall off and begin bouncing along the street. I remember other kids asking me if I was alright. The next thing I remember, I am in my classroom, and the teacher, washing the blood off my arms and face, asks me what happened. Not wanting to get my cousin in trouble, I said I fell in the schoolyard. After class, my cousin walked me home. Not wanting to face my mom, I immediately went to my bedroom. Not long after, my mom, with my cousin in tow, asked me what had happened. My cousin was worried and came over to see how I was doing. I spent the next four days in the hospital. Since it was the last week of school and I couldn't attend, I was still passed on to the next grade. Before the accident, I was near the top of my mathematics, spelling, and grammar class. By the start of the Fall semester, I was now in the middle of my class for mathematics. In addition, I became shy, especially around girls.

The second happens during a college-sponsored horseback riding event. It's a nighttime ride along the Chicago lakefront from Lincoln Park north to Montrose Hill. As club president, I had the bright idea to have our thirty-horse party circle Montrose Hill and charge to the top. This is exciting for our riders but not so much for the folks reclining on blankets watching the submarine races. We arrived at the top, regrouped, and rode back down to the bridal path amid yelling and screaming. Halfway down, the cinch on my saddle parted, dumping me onto the turf. I woke up in the arms of another rider. All I remember is her asking if I was all right.

The third TBI takes place at boot camp on the rifle range. The previous "prequal day," I fired a high expert. Consequently, unless I wanted to possibly get a lower 3 score on "qual day," I could assist in monitoring the targets of those still shooting. On this occasion, the recruits operating the targets were going slow, and the recruit trying to qualify may need more time. I turn to the Primary Marksmanship Instructor (PMI) and say, "Sergeant, they are screwing up on target eight." The PMI swings his target marker at me without looking at me, catching me above the left eye. I fell off the berm. Moments later, a Corpsman, the PMI, and my Senior Drill Instructor (SDI) asked me if I was all right. The SDI tells me that if this is reported, the PMI, who's just returned from Vietnam, could be in big trouble. So, no further action was taken, and I took one for the team.

Number four. During the riots in Pakistan, I was taking down the colors when a brick thrown over the embassy compound wall hit me in the head. I take the National Color into my arms and retire inside the embassy. No one else is in the embassy except for one secretary and me. I remain at my post until relieved at midnight. In the morning, the post-medical officer inspects my head and reports to my NCOIC I likely have a slight concussion. When the ambassador is made aware of the incident, he orders no official record that a local national caused the injury.

Number five is a self-inflicted injury brought about by incorrectly doing an exercise named Squat Thrusts. In this exercise, you stand at attention, legs shoulder length apart, squat until your palms are on the deck, and then kick your legs to the rear remaining in a front rest leaning position with your head thrown back. I was trying to see how many I could do in one minute. The result is whiplash that can be considered an mTBI. I'd just applied for Officer Candidates School, and an injury on my medical record could be disqualifying. So, I went to a private clinic for treatment.

And **number six** takes place while driving my city car, and I get t-boned. My vehicle is totaled and bent around the hood of the offending vehicle. I work my way out of the car before the traffic officer arrives. As I lean against the door, he asks how I feel just as my field supervisor arrives. Quoting city regulations and directions from our senior supervisor, and before asking me if I was OK, he directed me into his car and took me to a clinic for a drug test. Three hours later, I'm released to leave for the day. My favorite restaurant is across the street from headquarters. After dinner, I walk outside and cross the street to my car. The next thing I recall is waking up in the middle of the road with my head in the lap of a police sergeant asking me if I was OK.

###

Psychedelics

Recently, I spent the better part of the day speaking with Mental Health professionals at the VA on using psychedelics to treat PTSD/TBIs among both active duty and veterans. The discussion followed a recent article in **Veterans Health Care**, an online magazine:

Exploring psychedelics for the treatment of Veterans. September 26, 2023, By Hans Petersen

The premise is,

"When it comes to mental health, all options need to be on the table."

I'm old enough to remember the '60s when LSD and Magic Mushrooms were the drugs of choice for hippies and kook doctors.

One of my close doctor friends told me he recently received treatment with psychedelic drugs for his depression. And his wife, a Mental Health professional, also participated due to a months-long challenge with active suicidal ideation. I was taken aback.

You know me well enough that I had to do a deeper dive, if for no other reason than to set the record straight in my mind.

My initial conclusion is that this may be an option under a controlled, possibly one-time situation. However, there is limited evidence that this works and, more importantly, will not lead to substance abuse.

I remember when I was at UCLA Medical School, attending a two-week intense course on Drugs and Related Issues, that Methadone is used in medication-assisted treatment (MAT) to help people reduce or quit heroin or other opiates. My opinion is it switched one addiction for another.

My four-year success story pushing back against the challenges of mental health issues led me to believe that until medicine first exhausts non pharmaceutical remedies, the jump to psychedelics may not be the answer.

Hereditary Connection to PTSD

I keep returning to the movie **Patton** because it contains good and bad examples of leadership, mostly good and some not-so-good. In this particular clip, Patton is visiting the wounded in a field hospital, and you can see he is visibly moved by the seriousness of their wounds and by the sacrifices of his soldiers. As Patton moves along the cots, he comes to a soldier whimpering. Asking the soldier his problem, he says, "I guess I just can't take it, sir."

Although this incident is portrayed in WWII, recognizing the debilitating nature of combat-related PTSD remained in its infancy and was often misidentified by some leaders as cowardness. About twice as many American soldiers showed symptoms of PTSD during World War II than in World War I. This time their condition was called "psychiatric collapse," "combat fatigue," or "war neurosis."

Continuing my research, I came across some fascinating studies. One, in particular, "clearly suggests a predisposition or susceptibility for developing PTSD that is hereditary, with 30% of PTSD cases explained by genetics alone."

Using that information as a jumping-off point, I took a deeper dive into my family heritage to see if there was a pattern or set of circumstances to support that hypothesis.

On my birth father's side, my family arrived in Newfoundland, Canada, around 1639. As can happen on a close-quarters sea voyage, the brothers had a falling out, resulting in one heading to the Canadian interior and the other to the Massachusetts Bay Colony. Three generations later, 5th Great Grandfather Moses Spear settles outside present-day Boston and sees action in the Revolutionary War. The brother heading into Canada crosses into the USA in the early 1900s and starts farming in Michigan. At the onset of the Civil War, Great-Grandfather Edward joins a Michigan regiment and, after several engagements, is sent home. PTSD was not known then, so non-physical damage notes ``nostalgia." Edward uproots his family and leaves Michigan for Iowa, where he settles as a farmer. Papers submitted for his pension show no specific disorder, just a checkmark at "invalid."

My birth father served in the Pacific Ocean Theater on an aircraft carrier, the USS Hancock CVA-19, and after the ship saw service in many famous battles, he returned home. When he departed for the Navy, most agreed he was mild-mannered. Upon his return, now short-tempered, he beats my mom. After the divorce, he wanders West, landing in California, where he died in Federal prison in 1971. Recently, I discovered that his best friend, whom I am named after, also served on a carrier in the Pacific Theater. Arnold committed suicide in 1947.

My dad, the fantastic man that raised me, is one of three brothers serving in WWII. Dad is captured during the Ardennes battle and spends the remainder of the war as a POW in Germany. Dad was gregarious when he departed for war returning quiet, though now he doesn't mince words. Even if there is no direct hereditary 6 connection, growing up in an environment rife with obvious mental issues can impact a child negatively.

A significant drawback to writing this book is the number of family, friends, and casual acquaintances who will approach me recounting a story about their first-hand knowledge of a person who has committed or attempted suicide. In a few cases, the individual in the story is themselves.

I point out in the Disclaimer: "I am not a medical professional."

Consequently, my assistance often focuses on listening and offering examples of tools I have successfully used to hold back the specter of active suicidal ideation. At the same time, I must admit to myself and guard against periods of severe desolation this interaction can foster. These periods can last from a few minutes to hours, where my desire to write is completely blocked.

Recently, I completed the **Mental Health First Aid (MHFA)** Instructor course, an evidence-based training program administered by the National Council for Mental Wellbeing that teaches you how to identify, understand and respond to signs of mental health and substance use challenges.

Unintentional Experiment

Saturday, March 5th, 2022, presented me with the opportunity to, once again, use myself as a guinea pig, or some may say a "useful idiot."

On Saturday, I participated in a Lenten Retreat. It was great! I volunteered to purchase the meats, cheeses, croissants, and desserts. That's the first indicator that things are about to go sideways. Costco is a great place to shop; they place items at the entrance to get your attention and make your choices easier. So, as I first enter and to my immediate left are croissants. Eureka! I'm off to a great start. But, unfortunately, I didn't get fifty feet down the aisle and, what to my wondering eyes should appear, but **Sanders Dark Chocolate Sea Salt Caramels**. And, thinking only of my fellow retreatants, I bought them.

Arriving early, I meet up with our Hospitaller, who's busily sorting through the items she purchased for breakfast. Usually, I skip breakfast on my One Meal A Day (OMAD) regime, but once again, my eyes focus intently on two dozen Hot Cross Buns.

Aside from the Easter egg hunt, Hot Cross Buns were a real treat growing up in Chicago. No other time of the year will you see this delicious pastry in our house. Here they are, front and center, and I knew I shouldn't, but I did. In fact, along with the hot tea, I rescued two Hot Cross Buns. Each break saw me repeat the rescue, and I must admit, I began feeling self-satisfied. That should have been the first warning sign.

Lunch rapidly approaching, I repaired to the kitchen to lay out the meat, cheese, croissant, and dessert trays. Then, adding the chocolate caramels to a bowl, I convinced myself that if I took just one, what could it hurt—the second warning sign?

At lunch, I once again convinced myself that, although bread is not part of my ketogenic lifestyle, what would it hurt if I cheated and put the meat on a croissant, the third warning sign?

So, during lunch, and to remain sociable, I returned to the buffet for another sandwich AND two caramels-the fourth warning sign?

Later that evening, I ate my third meal of the day, which included meat and cheese from the retreat and two chocolate caramels. The fifth and last warning sign? What are all these warnings, and what is happening?

Getting a bit scientific, when we eat sweet foods, the brain's reward system — called the mesolimbic dopamine system, gets activated. Dopamine is a brain chemical released by neurons and can signal that an event is positive. When the reward system fires, it reinforces behaviors — making it more likely for us to carry out these actions again.

In my case, the Dopamine firing squad shot me five times, but I barely survived.

Retiring to my bed, dizzy, a bit disoriented, and slightly sick to my stomach as expected, I didn't sleep well, and aches and pains began to surface. You would think I was off the wagon if I hadn't just completed twenty-two days of my no-alcohol experiment.

Here are my takeaways from the weekend.

1. It's challenging to remain on any diet or lifestyle when faced with an abundance of foodstuffs you know are unhealthy.
2. Taking "just one" begins the slide down the slippery slope.
3. When you cheat, that's not the time to revert to a bad habit. Getting back on track is the key to success. Never give up, and start a fresh day.

January 31, 2023, was Day 30 in my no-alcohol experiment. So, to "celebrate," I joined my Malta friends at a local pub (Legends) following our monthly St Francis Home visit.

I ordered a pint of their Brown Lager and a plate of fish and chips. Then, wash it down with a second pint.

Back at the farm, I took my Blood Glucose, 107. This morning it was 79.

What are the overall results of my 30 days without alcohol?

1. I slept better-6/7 hours
2. I felt clearer in my mind
3. I lost 3 lbs
4. My skin is clearer

Going forward: I will continue to drink alcohol though less than before. I can't remember the last time I drank, intending to get drunk. But I do like the taste, especially with a good meal.

I am thinking about my next Guinea pig adventure. I am already low carb, high protein. Thirty days of keto/carnivore (beef, butter, bacon, and eggs) sounds interesting. The excellent start date is February 22nd, Ash Wednesday. How appropriate is that? I will add one glass of red wine for dinner. And, on Sunday, my usual 1 lb of shrimp.

My next semi-annual medical appointment is June 28, so I can get a complete blood/urine panel and see how it stacks up against previous lab results.

On what I thought would be my last research project, I started an experiment to coincide with the forty days of Lent.

Many will agree that New Year's resolutions don't pan out. The key reason is that it's a personal commitment where we hold only ourselves to account.

If we succeed, good on us. If we fail, oh well, try again next year.

So, I've decided to up the ante by tying this resolution to God.

After all, the best support anyone can expect comes from a commitment to improving ourselves by using the talents given to us by Our Creator. Do I expect to succeed? Yes. Do I have the will to succeed? Absolutely!

Up to this point, I have done well reworking my lifestyle and resolving physical and mental health issues. Since the lowest point just over three years ago, I've established a physical and psychological regime that's powerfully moved me toward my ultimate goal of a long, happy, healthy, and fulfilled life.

I want to take it to the next level by combining my skills and tying them to a specific duration that should showcase my success.

That period is Lent marking the 40 days that Jesus spent fasting in the desert, enduring temptation by Satan.

Let's get on to the resolution.

- ✓ I will stop drinking alcohol.
- ✓ I will start the Beginner Bodyweight Workout authored by Will Owen of Travel Strong.
- ✓ I will include at least one five-day water-only fast.
- ✓ When I eat, I'll continue the Ketovore lifestyle, mainly consisting of Beef, Butter, Bacon, and Eggs (BBBE).
- ✓ I will continue to follow an intermittent fasting One Meal A Day schedule. If I eat twice a day, it's in four hours.

For my part, I am entrusting my health and well-being to Jesus Christ the Great Physician.

This seven-week experiment proved to me that maintaining a strict "anything", especially where food, alcohol and physical training are concerned can be difficult, but is sustainable over the long term. I've included the blow-by-blow in the Appendix. It's quite revealing. In a nutshell, here are the...

Overall Lenten results:

Alcohol: I don't look forward to drinking as I did in the past. I'm just as refreshed with sparkling water.

Body workout: By increasing muscle mass, I have better balance and tone, and my emotional state benefits.

BBBE: I am not hungry; I feel good, with no aches and pains. That said, I will continue to eat non-starchy green vegetables. Weight down from 217 lbs seven weeks ago to 204 lbs. The belt size is 36 inches.

###

My research then surfaces several realities about why I've chosen the ketogenic metabolic lifestyle makeover: weight loss/maintenance, fewer aches and pains, reduction or elimination in both prescribed and over-the-counter drugs, and a clearer mind.

Keto and Mental Health

Although I started a strict keto regime of low carb/high fat in early 2020, I've found through further research that I can better understand what works for me by continuing to offer myself as the guinea pig. Although losing excess fat is an excellent bennie, it's the change in my mental health I'm most pleased to have strengthened.

For years, my PCP and I believed my problem was primarily mental. And the solution was drugs. Now, I am more convinced than ever the role of nutrition as it affects metabolic health is the critical player. The following is the tip of the iceberg of research I've done and continue to do to get myself right in the world.

In my journey to remain happy, healthy, and fulfilled, I found that many diets promote weight loss, but little about how you eat impacts your thoughts and emotions. So, I again turn to **Dr. Ken Berry, MD** and his many medical and scientific professional guests, looking for answers. They may only be in partial agreement but are willing to share their perspectives on the Low Carb Keto approach to optimal health.

One guest, Harvard-trained Psychiatrist **Dr. Georgia Ede, MD**, discusses her journey from a low-fat diet to Keto/Carnivore and its effect on mental health. Dr. Ede is among many traditionally trained practitioners pointing out that government Dietary Guidelines for Americans may be part of the problem rather than the cure for the decline in metabolic health. Specifically in obesity, type 2 diabetes, heart disease, stroke, kidney disease, and nonalcoholic fatty liver disease.

And a recent guest, **Dr. Christopher M. Palmer, MD**, also Harvard trained, authored a great book, ***Brain Energy***: A Revolutionary Breakthrough in Understanding Mental Health and Improving Treatment for Anxiety, Depression, OCD, PTSD, and More.

Interestingly, all three of the aforementioned MDs (Berry, Ede, and Palmer) searched for a non-drug intervention for their own physical and mental conditions. The result is a ketogenic lifestyle.

Earlier, I mentioned the ***Diet Doctor*** podcasts. Diet Doctor drills down into a topic in a way I can identify with, specifically on the issue of mental health. This podcast features **Dr. Shebani Sethi, MD**, a clinical assistant professor of psychiatry and behavioral sciences at Stanford University and founding director of the metabolic psychiatry clinic. She is at the forefront of the emerging field of metabolic psychiatry. Her research and clinical practice show the correlation between metabolic and mental health and the critical role of ketogenic diets as adjunctive therapy.

OK, let's tie it together with another Diet Doctor podcast; **Insulin resistance and why we get sick with Prof. Ben Bikman**. In his opening introduction, Dr. Bret Scher, MD, cardiologist and host for Diet Doctor, asks, "Is too much insulin a root cause for the chronic diseases that plague modern society?" He says, "According to Professor Ben Bikman, it likely is. And he should know. Professor Bikman is a scientist and researcher specializing in insulin and its effects on our health. In his new book, **Why We Get Sick**, Dr. Bikman makes a case for why we need to target insulin levels to improve global health. As you'll hear him say, lifestyle choices can cause insulin resistance, and they can cure it, too. The tools are at our disposal; we just need to know what they are and how to use them."

The entire interview surfaces that most general practitioners are likely behind the times in the literature, offering alternative therapies to treat disease. For example, although my primary care physician was supportive, he advised caution when I began the ketogenic lifestyle and closely monitored my blood work, but that's not always the case.

Lastly, a close friend and medical doctor said that doctors look at blood work as a marker for a problem, and as long as the numbers are within limits, no further action is needed. When I asked why that was, she replied, "We might have fifteen minutes between clients. After that, we don't have time to look for alternatives beyond the standard of care prescribed protocols."

###

Enter the Brain & Gut Connection

Back in the mid-70s, I was an intelligence analyst in Hawaii. I regularly presented analytical reports focused on the countries of interest in the command's area of responsibility. One such item reported that replacing one head of state for another would exacerbate an already tenuous situation and likely harm US relationships between the two countries. The Commander asked what I was basing my position on, and without thinking my response through, I said, "Sir, my gut tells me this is so." Later, my boss told me I should never admit an opinion is gut-related but instead based on solid analysis.

As it turns out, my gut instincts were correct.

Our guts send messages through the Vagus nerve to the brain when something isn't right. Some say it's a nervous, anxious, or even debilitating message to the brain telling the body to fight, flee or freeze.

Not all messages, at least on the surface, are harmful. Many directly respond to nutrients that stimulate the brain's pleasure receptors and signal we should eat. More; in my case, it's chocolate. Chocolate gives me a warm, soothing feeling in my stomach and a craving for more. Add salt, and I grab just one more piece of *Sanders Dark Chocolate Sea Salt Caramels.*

###

ALS and Keto I know I may sound like a snake oil salesman. Still, the ketogenic diet is long recognized as an effective treatment for pharmacoresistant epilepsy. And a growing body of literature supported by randomized clinical trials (RCT) suggests that the ketogenic diet could also be helpful in ALS, Alzheimer's, Parkinson's disease, and some mitochondriopathies.

In many ways, especially in the brain, a diet high in fats and low in carbohydrates reduces inflammation and protects nerve cells that significantly impact proper brain functioning.

A longtime Marine buddy and professional soccer referee has been diagnosed with ALS. He researched ALS and its impact on veterans. I was not surprised to read that his ALS RESOLUTION #630 was recently unanimously approved by the VFW National Convention, containing: ***"Whereas veteran suicide is a significant problem in our nation, the suicide rate for veterans with ALS is four times greater than for those without ALS,"***

I didn't question his assertion, but I had to dig deeper. When speaking with veterans diagnosed with PTSD and severely crippled by amputation, disfigurement, or stroke, I realized that the outwardness of their affliction greatly exacerbates their considering suicide.

By the very nature of an individual's chosen profession, be it the military, law enforcement, fireman, and first responder, the image in the general public's mind is one of a hero deserving acclaim. Unfortunately, the suffering of combat-related PTSD can often remain submerged, whereas a physical malady remains in plain sight. The once leaper of tall buildings in a single-bound Superman becomes a broken shell of their former self.

So, getting back to the ALS situation, why the high prevalence of suicide? I believe it's threefold.

1. One is that it's a death sentence. Approximately 80% of ALS patients die within two to five years.
2. Second, the debilitating effects are evident to everyone, family, friends, and the general public.
3. Lastly, the gradual downward spiral from significant other to an insignificant self who's now totally dependent could be perceived as a burden on those they love.

Against all odds, my Marine friend with ALS is still with us and MULE kicking ass. His spirits know no bounds. He remains active in sports and continues to make disparaging comments about naysayers in both public and private life. His belief in God, Corps, and Nation remains bolstered by a strong supporting cadre of family and friends.

It has been over three years since I began my physical and psychological makeover.

Throughout that period, I've continued to document my emotional state following the initial eating of sugar and then over the next twenty-four hours. My major takeaway is that when I eat sugar, especially chocolate cake, within minutes, I can tell my mood begins to swing. Initially, it's a nervous energy high, but later in the day or the following morning, thoughts of suicide begin to surface.

My journal entry from this morning (May 1, 2023) reads: *"I had a great meal last night at my daughter's. My Son-in-law grilled a fantastic brisket. I ate until I was pleasantly stuffed. I sampled the homemade potato salad but stayed with mostly asparagus. My downfall was the triple chocolate cake with frosting. I had two pieces. A couple and their two sons were present, and we talked until about eleven. I slept well and got up early for the ninety-minute ride back to the farm. Suddenly, I started thinking about suicide. My dogs usually travel with me, but I left them with my daughter because I'm going on a pilgrimage to Lourdes, France, for a week. Keeping that in mind, I rationalized that with them, not in the car, this would be an opportune time to have the tragic accident I'd planned years ago. I'm making this entry because I didn't do it."*

###

I've just returned from the Order of Malta's May 2023 week-long annual pilgrimage to Lourdes, France. During that week, knights, dames, volunteers, and our beloved Malades and their companions journey together, seeking a cure for their physical and psychological challenges. Consequently, my daily routine is drastically modified.

Eating more than one or two meals in a four-hour window is a radical change from my norm. It presents an ideal opportunity to closely monitor and support my previous "guinea pig" research showing a more likely than not correlation between what and when I eat and my mental health. Add to that the emotional events of the day, physically pulling or pushing the Malade in their carts, and the cumulative effect can be dramatic. So, I journaled each day and noted that, by day three, I struggled to maintain a happy, positive attitude.

A typical day's schedule went like this: Rise at 0600, breakfast at 0700, ready the carts at 0745, and travel to the morning's activities. Lunch at 1200, ready the carts at 1245, travel to the afternoon activities and return the malades to the hotel by 1700. Supper at 1900. Malades tucked in for the night by 2030. Team meeting to discuss the day's activities, often with adult libations. To bed between 2100-2400. Repeat.

What did I eat? Breakfast is usually eggs, bacon, ham, sausage, and tea. Although, I will admit I added a delicious chocolate pastry most days. For lunch and supper, we ate what was served. Except for one meal where I knew the meat was beef, the others were heavily sauced mystery meat. The sides were rice, carrots, potatoes, corn, or green beans. And there were always desserts. To remain social, I ate almost everything on my plate. My mom would be proud, but my mood began to change.

Activities included: Daily Mass, going to the baths, and stations of the cross, visiting local attractions, such as St Bernadette's home la Cachot (the prison), the Monastery of the Poor Clares, the château Fort de Lourdes and course, shopping. On the last full day, we traveled by bus into the countryside and the mountains to visit the town of Cauterets. Cauterets has been known for the virtues of its thermal waters for centuries. While still a small child, Bernadette contracted cholera and struggled with asthma. Bernadette's family often traveled there, hoping for a cure. They also attended church at Our Lady of the Assumption in the town.

Aside from scheduled activities, a connection may be established with a particular Malade or their companion and other Order members who either know I'm writing 23 this book or are looking for a compassionate ear. These interludes revealed the depth of their struggles, prescription drug abuse, family situations hampering full recovery, the suicide of a loved one, or thoughts of suicide themselves. My Saturday evening journal entry reveals I am becoming maudlin and need a change to remain focused.

I turned to my Team Leader and discussed the issue I was having with him. I'd become depressed, withdrawn, and hypersensitive during discussions or in my surroundings, and he listened nearly uninterrupted for an hour. Then, at one point, one of our chaplains approached. I explained the situation, and he gathered me in his arms and offered a heartfelt blessing.

At nearly 0100, I returned to my room and reread my journal entries from the previous days. The answer was right there before me. The likely culprit is a radical change in my eating regime when coupled with highly charged emotional interactions with others. I immediately changed back to meat, butter, bacon, and eggs. Cut all the sugar, carbs, sauces, and vegetables. By Monday evening, my mental outlook markedly improved. On Tuesday, I was back to my usual gregarious self.

In a discussion before embarking on the flight back home to Baltimore, my Team Leader commented on his amazement that I could self-assess to such a degree.

And that's the key not just for me but also for others. Too often, we blindly accept the directions or suggestions of others, whether medical professionals, family, or friends, on how to deal with physical or emotional challenges. In my case, I refuse to blindly accept that another pill, psychotherapy, or stiff upper lip attitude can remedy my challenges. Instead, I'm researching, keeping good notes, and always asking, **"Why."**

Chapter 9
An Early Love of Animals

Nearly all of my animals are rescued. When choosing a companion animal, it's like getting a new roommate. You can go the new puppy route or go to the animal shelter and search among the many animals needing adoption. And I've done both. It may surprise you, but rescue programs often showcase large animals. The Bureau of Land Management (BLM) regularly disposes of wild horses and donkeys. How much does adopting or purchasing a wild horse or burro cost? An untrained wild horse or donkey's minimum adoption or purchase fee is **$25**. The fee applies to events using a lottery draw or a first-come, first-serve method. Some adoptions use competitive bidding and can have a higher adoption fee.

Going the puppy route, you can finely hone the characteristics sought: size, shedding, not shedding, good with children, or best as a guard dog. Older rescues often have a pedigree: health, expected longevity, social history, and likely house broken.

Living in the countryside, I always wonder when the opportunity to add to my family will appear. Ditch is a collie found by my daughter as she drove along a country road at night. She stopped initially because of what appeared to be two puppies. Both were dead. Turning toward her car, she heard whining from the nearby ditch. TaTa...Ditch!

Holly, the coon hound, is another of my daughter's finds. Again, driving toward the farm at night, she saw a small dog scamper in front of the car. Stopping, she gathers the only weeks-old dog up on Christmas Eve.

Cats are another story. You either love them or not, and vice versa. Living here at the farm can be a challenge for a cat. If raised here, they develop a second sense of danger. Curiosity about a poisonous snake is fatal if brought from a city or primarily in-house environment.

###

In 2021, I received an early Christmas present. Friday evening, it was sleeting, and Raider and I were relaxing in the parlor. Raider alerted me to something, so we got up, and I followed him to the back door. I opened the door and found these two dogs. I live in hunting country, so it's common for dogs that may not hunt, be beyond their prime, or just unwanted to be dropped off to fend for themselves. So, since they didn't have collars and I couldn't see them in the dark, I closed the door. I didn't sleep well that night and hoped they wouldn't still be there. As I left the house in the morning, I found them huddled under a large English Boxwood near my back door. Again, I know they won't go away if I feed them. I put Raider into my car and took him with me to church. The temperature was going into the high 60's, and I wasn't worried about the dogs. But, if they were still there when Raider and I returned, I needed another plan. They were there patiently waiting on the back porch. They barked, whined, and moved farther into the porch as I approached them. It was early afternoon, so I made a drink, grabbed my book, and sat in the yard. The dogs didn't come, and Raider ignored them. That evening I broke the rule about feeding strays.

Sunday morning, they remained huddled under the bush. Fed them alongside Raider (who growled when they approached his bowl), and I left for Mass. Returning, all three dogs were in the yard, though respectfully at a distance from each other. Sunday is a treat day for Raider, and he knows it.

So, I went into the barn and dragged out an Igloo doghouse, some extra bowls, and a large doggie bed from the family room. I retrieved three marrow bones, gave one to Raider, and attempted to coax the dogs off the porch and into the crate. After several minutes they approached close enough to lick the bone and my fingers but wouldn't enter the Igloo. Happily chewing their bones, I left all three in the backyard. When evening feeding time arrived, I put food into their bowls and threw a handful inside the Igloo.

Monday morning, they were huddled together inside the Dog Igloo.

The two now had a home. They are very young, inseparable girls with no ticks, fleas I can see, or apparent injuries. I have an appointment with the Vet for Raider on 2 January sixth. I intend to take them for a complete checkup. Oh, BTW...their names are Lady Mutt & Lady Jeff.

Murphy's Eighth Law is: If everything seems to be going well, you've obviously overlooked something.

Initially, I was fortunate to have Ladies Mutt and Jeff find Raider and me a few days before Christmas. They are only three months old. As we became acquainted, Lady Jeff chased me down the driveway and got hit by a car. I immediately took her to my vet: fractured right front and right rear leg. Except for the cut, all else looked good, so I took her to the emergency Vet in Richmond. Unfortunately, no surgeons are available till after January third. So, she will stabilize till then.

I patiently waited for a call from the surgeon. He reports that each fracture is within growth sections of the bone, with no apparent damage to joints. Initially, the surgeon suggested doing both surgeries under one anesthesia; if the first one went well, she could be home 36-48 hours following surgery with 4-6 weeks of crate rest and limited outside activity.

Once the surgeon opened her legs up, he determined one would have to be amputated. So, Lady Jeff would be a tripod. Unfortunately, not five minutes later, the surgeon called back and reported the rear leg was also not salvageable. Since she was under anesthesia, my sweet little girl was put to sleep. I miss her terribly.

Raider, my service dog I've mentioned, I haven't properly introduced. Raider travels with me just about everywhere. Raider is also a rescue, though I didn't know it when I got him. Before Raider, there was Captain Jack, my pug. When Captain Jack died of the rare red blood disease, I knew the void as my service dog needed to be filled, but I wasn't sure what breed. During a visit to a friend living in the mountains of western Virginia, she mentioned that a local hunter had a litter of 3 puppies looking for a home. Was I interested? Within an hour, the hunter brought the puppies to her house. In the crate were nine three-week-old Australian Cattle Dog/Beagle mix puppies. And I was getting the pick of the litter. Checking them over, I decided on the most active and colorful. The hunter said he would have the puppy checked out at the vet, get all the shots, and return the puppy to me at six weeks old. I decided to name the puppy after my son, a Marine Raider. TaTa-Raider. Good to his word, the hunter returned with Raider and gave me his shot record.

I mentioned Raider is a rescue. This combined breed may be good at herding cattle, but they won't hunt. I learned a few weeks later that the hunter had killed the other eight puppies. I wish I had known I would have taken them all and found good homes for them.

Raider can detect when someone is lonely or emotionally disturbed. At that time, he will walk over to the person, lean against their leg, and look up as if to say, "It's OK. I am here." Raider is a big hit when I take him on pilgrimage, conferences, or sailing. On many occasions, I will be approached and asked if Raider can go for a walk or sit next to a conference participant. There is an immediate connection and a mutual display of love and caring. Sailboat racing is another opportunity for Raider to showcase his skills. Whenever a sailor asks if Raider can ride on their boat during a race, that boat often finishes in the top three. I am not the only one lucky to have him in my life.

I had no idea a rattlesnake could strike that fast.

My parents were concessionaires working at the Lincoln Park Zoo in Chicago. Too young to sell souvenirs, I spent Sundays exploring the many animal and reptile exhibits. The small mammal house stood next to my father's stand. I became a mascot to the zookeepers, and, over several years, I was allowed to handle, feed and interact with their charges.

A special friend of mine is Judy, the elephant. Although not a small mammal, Judy spent winters in a large indoor cage and an open outdoor enclosure during milder weather. As a result, I became adept at working with many species, developing a deep appreciation for their variety and idiosyncrasies.

An extra attraction for me was the *Zoo Parade TV Show*, filmed at the Zoo. The host is Marlin Perkins, the director of the Zoo. His son, Freddy, and I became friends and often trailed along during the show's shooting.

During a pre-rehearsal for the show, Freddy and I were close by when, as Marlin reached for the timber rattlesnake using a long snake hook, the snake shot along the stick, biting him in the hand. That got my attention.

Dr. Marlin Perkins left Lincoln Park for the directorship of the St. Louis Zoo and later went on to host the *Mutual of Omaha Wild Kingdom* TV Program.

My love for handling most animals and reptiles came in handy as a Boy Scout Camp Counselor.

So, in the realm of companion animals, although I have many to pick from, I prefer dogs, cats, and horses because they can establish attachments beyond a food source.

On the Sundays I spent at the zoo, I often went to a playground near the bridal path that circumnavigates the park. The cinder track goes along Lake Michigan to Montrose Harbor, circling Montrose Hill, a magnet for folks gathering on the hill to watch the submarine races. Often, I watched the many horseback riders cantering along. I'm hooked!

That summer, I attended the American Boys Camp in Wisconsin. We lived in cabins, ate in a converted barn, learned to swim, rowed boats, and rode horses. Well, they were ponies. One day, I returned to the riding ring to feed carrots to the ponies during my free time. On this occasion, I arrived before the riding instructors. Full of more piss than common sense, I got a pony close to the fence and jumped on.

Unfortunately, I lasted long enough to be thrown through the fence. I returned with bruised ribs and a damaged ego when the instructor was present the following day. I am hooked again!

The next step up is from ponies to HORSES. Back at Lincoln Park stables, I spent one night a week learning how to groom, tack, and feed the horses properly, including mucking out the stalls. Then, one day, my dad visited to see the grand draw. As I curried a beautiful Chestnut, I pointed down the line of stalls and asked Dad what he could see. His response reveals, "A bunch of stalls, horses, and girls."

Ah, the light comes on-girls.

College provides another opportunity to enjoy riding. So I joined the Boots and Saddles Riding Club. The then-president is popular, a natural leader, and his parents own a dude ranch in Northern Illinois. So naturally, our club activities centered around the ranch.

I was elected president in my second year and moved our club back to Lincoln Park for nighttime rides. One night we had over thirty horses in the group. Remember Montrose Hill?

Circling the hill and on my signal, we charged to the top amid many folks lying on blankets watching the "submarine races." They are not happy. So, to add insult to injury, I gathered my riders on the hilltop and charged back down. Unfortunately, my cinch broke during the charge, and I crashed to the ground. I awake to Mary, my head in her lap, asking if I'm OK. One more TBI to the growing list of head injuries.

I've often managed to have a horse while on active duty, even when assigned to our embassy in Pakistan. The available horses are often former polo ponies, and I regularly rode a spirited Chestnut. I have a thing for Chestnuts.

Alongside my service dog, Raider, I've owned four horses in the past decade. Hank was an old boy and well past his prime. The kids loved to ride him because he was so gentle and knew the way home should the rider forget or fall off. My granddaughter showed an interest in horses, and I was pleased. I jumped at the opportunity when the stable owner indicated Hank was for sale. The owner cautioned me that Hank often came up lame, and if I didn't buy him, he would likely be disposed of. Hank and she rode together happily for several years. Now bitten by the competitive riding bug, she needs a new horse.

Although Sir Henry wasn't new, he was a spirited Mustang with a mind of his own. At her first novice competition, she and Sir Henry entered the jumping ring, and before even starting, Sir Henry turned out of the ring and cantered over to a donkey joyfully braying at the fence. Still, when Sir Henry behaved, he provided sufficient saddle time for my granddaughter to advance. My third horse is Tiger Lily. She is a beautiful blond-tan and perfect for moving to the next level, and she has already been placed several times at recognized shows. Recently, a judge observed Tiger Lily had difficulty negotiating three rail jumps at a show. After the show, we had the vet check, and she has Proximal Suspensory Desmitis, which in layman's terms, is a sudden onset of lameness that usually improves in a few days. Tiger Lily will be leased out to novice riders.

Consequently, in our search for the next horse to support my granddaughter's climb up the eventing ladder, we have settled on a twelve-year-old May Mays Cat, sired by Rutledge Cat, in the line of Secretariat. "Steve," his barn name, continues to grow with my granddaughter as they work out each other's eccentricities.

Although I don't ride English, I may return to riding Western. However, my most profound involvement is being with the horses at the many shows, inhaling the sweet essence of horses (manure, sweat, leather, and hay).

As stated earlier, dogs are great, but horses are powerful.

How, then, do companion animals and horses significantly impact my PTSD?

First and foremost, I am responsible for most of their upkeep: stabling, vet visits, tack, and training. It's a deep commitment to the horse and someone you love when you take on these responsibilities. Day to day, their success is your success.

A brochure I distribute at shows invites riders and owners to consider riding as therapeutic recreation.

My involvement in the therapeutic recreation arena spans over a quarter-century.

If you are a horse owner, operate a stable, or are interested in horses as companion animals, here's how you can do it.

I have a well-grounded appreciation for what is required to integrate individuals with disabilities (especially veterans) into a professionally established therapeutic recreational program.

Here are three options you may want to consider:

1. Most folks are well acquainted with dogs as companion animals. Still, horses, too, can be central to a participant's continued well-being. While some veterans can no longer comfortably ride, they can enjoy being in the company of horses and those with a similar affinity.
2. As it relates explicitly to PTSD, the closeness of the horses and watching riders go through their paces when riding or caring for the horse can improve a veteran's mental health.
3. Another option to consider is to broaden the reach of your facility and program to reach a more extensive client base by offering equine-assisted activities and therapies through organizations such as:
    a. **PATH International** https://www.pathintl.org/path-intl-centers/join-now and,
    b. **Hoofbeats Therapeutic Riding Center** https://www.hoof-beats.com Hoof-Beats is located right here in Lexington, Virginia.

Won't you join me as we explore how to remove blinders and open up a new world of possibilities for Our Veterans?

Chapter 10
Remaining Active is Critical

Saturday mornings

I have always been a morning person, even as a child. So Saturday mornings, while my parents were still in bed, you could find me with my face glued to our 13-inch TV screen. First is Winky-Dink and You, followed by Howdy Doody. Then, at 10:00, the movies began, primarily Westerns and, on occasion, dramas.

One of the actors I remember from many movies is George Sanders. I found Sanders the epitome of a cultured, often rude, and always in control actor. During an interview, Sanders, when asked if there was any part left he would like to play, replied, "Well, no one has ever asked me to play God. I suppose that's what I would like."

In the early nineteen seventies, I was shocked to see on the TV news that Sanders, age 65, had committed suicide, leaving a note: "Dear World, I am leaving because I am bored."

Ultimately, Sanders got his desire to play God by ending his own life.

###

If boredom can be a possible cause of suicide, wouldn't an active lifestyle be a good remedy?

And, if ***"Idle Hands Are the Devil's Workshop,"*** then couldn't depression, anxiety, and suicide be among the Devil's best sellers?"

I have found that I am happiest and healthiest when I remain active. Therefore, my calendar reflects recurring opportunities I look forward to each month, and I am always looking for additional activities to ensure my life remains fresh.

So, what will you see if you look over my shoulder at my calendar?

First, the majority of the days will include Mass. I not only attend church, but I am also an Altar Server. Church, for me, is an anchor providing stability should I become maudlin. It's an opportunity to be in His presence. As the Divine Physician, Jesus is always ready to listen and positively influence my turbulent life. I'm often amazed at how hearing the Word of God through Scripture can solve a current problem or one lurking in the background.

Secondly, I have recurring commitments as a Knight in the Order of Malta. First Friday Mass. Second Wednesday at St. Peter's feeding the homeless, and the third Tuesday at St. Francis Home, where we gather in the Chapel for Adoration and prayer before we walk the halls selling cookies and cheese sticks to the residents. The cost. A smile. If I say these opportunities are humbling, that would hardly cover the emotional connection with those we serve: our Lords, the sick, and the poor.

Some activities I enjoy are more seasonal or require focused planning.

I have always been an active hiker. Boy Scouts, the Marines, and any opportunity to get away all jump-start a desire to walk long distances. Following my retirement from the Corps in 1988, I held a few satisfying full-time jobs in the civilian sector. At the time, I still hadn't been diagnosed with PTSD, and walking was a great way to remove me from the stress of being with people daily. So in 1996, I found myself again without a steady job and planned to thru-hike the Appalachian Trail (ATC). All 2,164 miles of it from Springer, Georgia, to Baxter State Park and Mt. Katahdin, Maine. Total time on the trail is five months and four days. I would not do it a second time. **Awarded the ATC 2,000-miler tab.**

###

I travel the USA between April and August to certify sailing instructors for US Sailing. These classes run over three days and often coincide with weekends or holidays. Add in two travel days, and my schedule can fill up rapidly. The classes are intense, and I must be spot on when explaining or demonstrating specific skill sets. In recognition of my efforts, I was **Honored by the Community Sailing Council of the United States Sailing Association "for extraordinary Outreach and Inclusion in the effort to make sailing accessible to both general and special publics."**

###

Activities that require more detailed planning are the annual pilgrimages.

The Order of Malta, pilgrimage to the National Shrine of Our Lady of Champion in Wisconsin, is always the first weekend in August. And the Order's week-long pilgrimage to Our Lady of Lourdes in France begins the first Wednesday in May. This pilgrimage brings as many as 8,000 Knights, Dames, and volunteers together as we host our malades seeking spiritual, and, hopefully, physical healing at the baths in the Grotto.

More serious planning is required as I pilgrimage to the Camino de Santiago in Spain, the Via Francigena in Italy to St Peter's Square in Rome, the St. Magnus Way on the Island of Orkney in Scotland, and the Holy Land.

I prefer to walk these pilgrimages solo. I've found if I am not in a group, it increases the opportunities to meet exciting fellow pilgrims and has additional time to remain at one point of interest or pass another by. The exception is the Holy Land. A skilled guide is indispensable to gaining access to requisite shrines and locations.

Your physical conditioning is a significant consideration. Again, taking my Primary Care Physician's word, I have physical laboratory results similar to a healthy man in his sixties. Remaining physically fit is crucial because you often carry everything you need on your back. I have walked the Camino seven times. Twice from St Jean Pied de Port, France, to the cathedral of Santiago, Spain (790 km/490 miles).

When asked why I prefer to walk alone, I'll respond, "Just as I like to be a hermit when at home, when I walk long distances, I can escape into a world of personal decision-making and overcoming obstacles."

Still, there are times when being alone can be a two-edged sword.

I mentioned physical conditioning is needed to make these long hikes. A key benefit is that if you accidentally slip off a ridge knife-edge, misstep crossing a boulder field, or get stung by a wasp, each has happened to me. It's good conditioning that can make a difference in your survival.

I no longer lift heavy weights or do cardio. So, in preparation, my focus now is on **Bodyweight Workouts**. I don't need more than a mat and a location. Keeping your muscles strong and flexible increases balance and reduces injuries from falls.

Lastly, fatigue, dehydration, and loss of electrolytes can add up to convincing yourself that you are still on the correct trail.

All of this cost me dearly on the *Via Francigena* in 2022. The temperature was in the high 90s, and I had just reached a stage where I was less than an hour from my destination for the day. With less than a quart of water remaining, I took a left instead of a right. Initially, I was pleased the trail was heading in a straight line and downhill. Moving along quickly, I became concerned that I hadn't recently observed a trail marker.

Taking out my iPhone, I checked the GPS, and sure enough, I was nearly two miles off course. Retracing my steps and taking the correct turn added three hours before I arrived at my hostel for the night.

Here are two additional examples of bad situations.

On the Appalachian Trail, I'm traversing a bald ridge in Virginia. Most of the day is pleasant but May can develop severe thunderstorms. Seeing the clouds build up, I checked my map for the closest shelter, which was only a mile away down the hill. A torrential downpour follows the first clap of thunder as I step under the eve of the six-person shelter. I lay out my sleeping bag and stretch my tarp across the mouth of my den of the evening.

The supper is finished, and the dishes are cleaned and stowed away. I removed the shelter's register from its waterproof folder. Initially, my entry only speaks of the day's fifteen-mile hike, with the only point of interest being the rattlesnake I crossed earlier sunning itself on a ledge. The rain continues unabated, and my mood resembles the menacing clouds above. The register entry continues. I am nearly out of food, but by noon tomorrow, I will reach the trail town post office and retrieve my next package sent by my wife.

My wife. Well, no longer my wife. She and I divorced two years back, and she is now married to Jim. Just thinking of what I have lost sends my heart beating in time with the raindrops striking upon the roof. Moving into a corner well away from the misting spray, I drape my poncho across everything; hugging myself, I cry. I don't remember any thoughts of suicide, but I did have a profound sense of loss.

A quarter-century later and thousands of miles away, I am again a pilgrim walking **the Way** to the Cathedral of Santiago in Spain. Over my previous six treks on the Camino, I have made several friends in Spain, and this particular stop in 2021 is high on my list to spend a few days before pressing on.

Typically, both the pilgrims and locals get along. There are exceptions, and this is one. As is my wont, Sunday Mass is necessary, and I am joining several local folks.

Walking to the church, the question of why I am on Camino comes up, and I explain it's an opportunity to leave my cares behind and grow stronger in my faith. One of the folks wears yellow-tinted glass, and I know Spaniards can be avid hunters. When I suggest the connection, it's clear the man is against gun ownership by civilians.

After Mass, we go to the local bar for a beer and lunch. I'm asked if I fought in Vietnam. I answer in the affirmative. This sets off a diatribe focused on me. He calls me a murderer. Not finished, he says I should just kill myself and rid the earth of my scum.

I couldn't sleep that night and rose well before the others; I walked off into the night. I am so shaken I can hardly walk or think straight. Not trusting myself to walk alone, at the next town, I board the train and, surrounded by others, ride to the next central town where there will be medical assistance should I need it.

Among the many positives to my walking, here is a beautiful memory from the *Appalachian Trail*.

The temperature is approaching 100 degrees as I arrive at a twelve-person shelter high on a Pennsylvania ridge. Normally I'd walk another hour or two, but I am nearly out of water, and three springs are near this site. I drop my pack in the corner of the shelter and move downhill two hundred yards to the first water point. It's dry. Further along the steep trail, the second is also dry. I am over a quarter mile from the shelter when the sound of water rushing along the stone spring bed immediately perks me up. Filling my two Nalgene bottles, I start the long steep climb back to the shelter.

Less than an hour later, I hear movement off to my left along the ridgeline. It's a group of twelve Mennonite women wearing traditional Kapp, dresses and carrying heavy packs. As the leader sees the shelter is occupied and not answering my greeting, she leads them downhill to the water point. I yell out there's no water until the third stream. The last two in the gaggle are still in their teens. Waving to me as they pass, they thank me for the information.

Not thirty minutes later, the ladies return, and the leader nods in my direction. I blurted out that I'm happy to leave the shelter to them, but she says they have tents and they will move to the nearby meadow. The sun now sets, and I can hear beautiful singing. My mood lightens, and I thank God for little graces. Again, I hear rustling, and the ladies have returned to stand in front of the shelter. Their voices joined with my happiness for several minutes as they serenaded me. Gosh, aren't trail angels great?

Metal Detecting

Another favorite pastime is metal detecting. I began this as a recreational physical exercise when stationed in Hawaii. It didn't take long to realize beaches contained a treasure trove of dropped coins, keys, and lost jewelry.

My year-long assignment in Okinawa offered another valuable opportunity. I brought my underwater metal detector. It's lightweight and easily fits into my baggage. Adding SCUBA to my activities, I had an arrangement with a local Japanese resort that allowed me to detect as long as I removed any trash I found. There are few tourists during winter, so I donned my wetsuit and made ten ninety-minute dives. Recovered: over $4,000 in jewelry, nearly $800 in coins, and assorted sunglasses, watches, and a Sake set.

Here in Virginia, I have access to many stately 17th-century homes and Civil War-era sites where relics can be found, such as heirloom jewelry, fired and dropped bullets, uniform hardware (buttons, buckles, breastplates), camp utensils, cannon balls, and artillery shells.

Not highlighted on my calendar though it should be, is my writing.

I've written many directed think pieces and intelligence summaries through the years. Although I enjoy researching and crafting these documents, it is work. That doesn't stop me from writing for fun and profit. I've written several articles for magazines and published a factional novel, **Merchant's List**, under my pen name A.N. Caird.

When folks who know me well, especially those I served with, read **Merchant's List,** they are convinced it is autobiographical. And indeed, I draw heavily from past experiences.

An example is **in the Prologue**.

"Three days later, the squad returned to the command post. Alan was relieved to be back in the safety and comfort of the base. He had been feeling sick, not sick to his stomach, but in his heart and soul. He knew exactly what he needed, so he sought out the chaplain, Father Bob. The two men had a heartfelt conversation in the sanctity of the base's chapel.

Alan began to experience emotions that were uncommon to him. He cried.

"So, was this your first mission with confirmed kills?" the Priest asked as he began his inquisition.

Alan looked up through his teary eyes and winced as he released a long, exaggerated exhale. This response was enough to answer the question.

"Look, better them than you." Father said as he placed his right hand on Alan's shoulder to comfort his grief."

Chapter One reflects on where Alan finds himself and could reveal a subconscious thought about suicide.

"Prayer is not always a fixed combination of litany learned by rote. So often, prayer is more of a conversation with God that doesn't require spoken words. But this morning, alone with God, Alan decides to speak aloud.

"God, I've had an epiphany. If you take me right now, I am ready to go home."

"Ready to go home." Alan whispers.

Once more, settling even deeper and centering himself... inhale... exhale... inhale... notice the passing thoughts and slowly send them on their way... inhale... exhale...

Is he really at that point in his life where he believes nothing is left to be done?...inhale...Is his bucket list now crumpled and discarded into a round circular file?... exhale... Is there no one left in his life worth living for? Who will surely miss him?"

###

Soccer

I have been involved in "the beautiful game" since 1974 when I coached my son on a U-5 Boys team in Hawaii. That is also the beginning of nearly a half-century as a soccer official. I've participated as a referee, instructor, and assessor. Following an incapacitating injury in 2000, I retired my boots and served at the highest professional level as a National Assessor. Another medical malady sidelined me in 2018. This year, 2023, I returned to soccer as a Referee Coach. Among my awards is induction into the **Virginia Intercollegiate Soccer Officials Association Hall of Fame.**

###

Movies

I've already commented on how the movie ***Patton*** contains snippets of his actions that impacted my life. During my youth and as a reward for good grades and doing my chores, I could go to the movies on Saturday afternoons. Watching movies can imbed valuable moral lessons and set one on a future career path.

For example, my desire to become a Marine is likely due to watching films such as The ***Sands of Iwo Jima***. Aside from John Wayne's portrayal of Sergeant Stryker and how he molds his Marines into a credible fighting force, the value of their formed interpersonal relations is genuinely remarkable.

Another ***God is My Co-pilot***, an autobiographical war film by Robert Lee Scott. It recounts his service with the Flying Tigers

145

and the US Army Air Forces in WWII. Unlike the fictional Sgt Stryker, Colonel Scott is a real-life action figure.

I've mentioned all my dogs are rescues, and **Old Yeller** reveals that a "stray dog," when accepted as a family member, can result in lifesaving actions, even to the point of sacrificing themselves. Raider, my service dog, is a testimony to that fact.

This Independence Day (2023), I returned to the big screen after several years to watch the movie **Sounds of Freedom** starring Jim Caviezel.

And the movie resurfaced some old wounds I thought were deeply buried. The movie's location is primarily set in Colombia and Honduras, but my involvement in human trafficking is in Central Africa, particularly South Sudan.

In the mid-1980s, I was part of a four-man anti-terrorism unit headquartered at US Central Command in Tampa, Florida. Although we moved throughout the CentCom Area of Responsibility (AOR), the southern region of Sudan held my attention for many reasons; not the least: it sits astride the ivory smuggling route and is vital to Islamist militant groups traveling between East and North Africa. During the fact-finding visits to the region, I became intimately aware of the savagery perpetrated against the majority Christian population in the Darfur province and critical cities of Juba and Nimule.

Human traffickers exploit domestic and foreign victims in South Sudan, and traffickers use victims from South Sudan abroad. These vermin compel victims to engage in commercial sex and work in legal and illicit industries and sectors.

According to the census, the states of Virginia, Washington, Maryland, California, Idaho, Minnesota, and North Carolina have the largest Sudanese populations in the US.

The South Sudanese population I came into contact with was all about the family unit as central to their daily lives. They were strong in their Christian beliefs and would go out of their way to be gracious hosts. On one specific occasion, they made me aware of a possible threat and strongly suggested I retire from the area.

At the theater watching **Sound of Freedom**, I sat next to a twelve-year Army veteran. As the previews rolled by, I mentioned my appreciation for how difficult it is to honestly combat human trafficking when it's a $150 billion revenue-generating source for individuals and governments.

He and his wife listened closely and asked some excellent questions that I did my best to answer. My final takeaway was that although historical slavery is thousands of years old and my contract is forty years in the past, little has changed to end this blight.

In **Sound of Freedom**, two children, central to the story, were abducted and sold into prostitution (Miguel 10 years old) and Coca leaf processing/sex slave (Llanto early teens). Today, across the world, children work for pennies an hour so that you can save a few dollars at the cash register.

I've thought long and hard about whether I should include this, but...well, here goes.

The movie **Sound of Freedom** centers on trafficking in children. What about trafficking in adults?

Although the ages of these adults can go well into senior years for domestic and semi-skilled positions the majority are in their late teens. There are international companies that will provide the customer a "legal" companion for a steep fee.

By the time I was mid-career in the Marines, I'd traveled worldwide and considered myself fairly sophisticated, though not always accepting, of a particular nation's cultural proclivities. And, on this occasion, I was cautioned not to get involved.

Our team was midway through a two-month-long assignment in the Middle East and East Africa. Today we were again taking a breather in one of the highly trafficked regional airline hubs. And we found ourselves in a popular British pub populated by many nationalities. I may have mentioned I was at one time a skilled enough dart player to seldom have to pay for drinks, and I did often bring home the prize turkey.

This evening, I was nearly the turkey.

There were six boards in action, and I found myself next to a Saudi dressed in a traditional thobe. He wasn't throwing all that well and was becoming highly agitated. Sitting behind him on a stool was a very attractive young lady. By her appearance and accent, I thought she was English. She was well-dressed and displayed a lot of gold jewelry. Watching the interaction between the two it was obvious they were together.

At one point, the Saudi tossed a double eight to win the match. When he turned to celebrate, he saw his female companion facing away and talking to another man. Incensed, he struck the girl forcefully enough to knock her to the floor.

I rushed forward to strike the a-hole but was restrained. Our local counterpart informed me that the girl was the Saudi's property, and he could do as he wished. For the girl's part. She may remain in the relationship for one, maybe two years max. Her reward-she will likely accumulate more money in cash and jewelry than she could make in twenty years back home.

As the world turns my friends.

I don't have an answer. Yet, there are those who espouse the answer is a one-world government. The UN was touted as the answer where all member nations could meet peacefully to settle disputes, and end war, poverty and human trafficking.

How's that working out?

Reading a good book

Just to relax, I enjoy sitting in my favorite leather chair with a good book. I'm not looking for deep-thinking documentaries or novels. I'd instead escape into a land of dragons, kings and queens, elves, dwarfs, and magicians. Fantasy is a far cry from the first book I checked out at the library in fifth grade— the Children's Rise and Fall of the Roman Empire.

Music

For the majority of my life, I've enjoyed music. Throughout my teens, it was whatever was popular, and I knew all the words. In college, I slipped into classical music to quiet my emotions before a particularly tough test, and the go-to piece was Czech composer Bedřich Smetana's most famous tune, *"The Moldau."*

In Vietnam, I had a small 45-rpm battery-powered record player I carried around. There were a few records to choose from, with the Association's *"Cherish"* and the Beatles *"Yellow Submarine"* topping the list. I often got into trouble for taking the batteries from our unit field phone. In Pakistan, I was the hit of most parties because I had the only copy of the Beatles' *"White Album"* and Simon and Garfunkel's *"Sounds of Silence."*

If music can soothe the savage beast, my favorite when assigned to the Anti-terrorist unit is *Canon in D* by Pachelbel. I mentioned our team leader is a no-nonsense bulldog of an Army Ranger Colonel, and one evening in Khartoum, Sudan, he takes out a small cassette player and pops in cello music. The first up is Canon in D. I'm hooked.

Over the years, I've gone through phases, but most often return to '60s and '70s pop music, Niel Diamond, and Heart.

A close friend following my road to the Light recently recommended I watch a music video by Bailey Zimmerman, *"Religiously."* I value her insight, so I followed up with the following email to her.

"Close friend,"

I sincerely appreciate *Religiously*.

I listened to it three times. Once to read the lyrics. Second to find the message. Lastly, to see if I needed those tissues you mentioned. No, but the message came through and I found a bit of me there and a lot of my "wife."

Buoyed by this success of not becoming too emotional over music (I no longer play music on long drives). I tried an experiment. I liked to shuffle the genre. Rock, 60s/70s and Country.

There is one song that always made me pull over and stop the car. I'd hear the first notes and rapidly lose it emotionally.

My daughter knows if I text her "Heart" I am blubbering somewhere, and she will wait until I text her "I am OK."

So, the experiment. Hoping I no longer was so tightly wound I played "Alone."

It's good I was alone. The raw emotion came back with a vengeance. I cried and kept saying to my wife, "I am so sorry... I'm so sorry!" Some might say I failed the experiment because the hoped-for result was, I could get through Alone...alone.

I consider it a success.

My favorite lyrics:

Till now I always got by on my own
I never really cared until I met you
And now it chills me to the bone
You don't know how long I have wanted
To touch your lips and hold you tight
You don't know how long I have waited
And I was going to tell you tonight

"Close friend", it's when I am alone, I am most vulnerable.

That's why I read about kings, elves, dwarfs and dragons. To escape into a place where nothing is real and good triumphs over evil.

When I would warn my wife about my concern over her relationship with Jim, before I knew how far it had progressed, I would tell her ***"The dragon has been released."*** And she should just stay away for a while. I would walk away and go somewhere alone and cry my eyes out.

"Close friend", thank you for being there. You don't know the extent of the positive impact our talks have on me. My clinician is my clinical friend. You are an important friend. Thanks for being there and thinking of me.

Arn and Raider

PS. I'm going to try Alone one more time. Though tonight is likely the last time for a long time. A

Social Media

Being on social media is another avenue to walk down at your own risk. Again, this is where you expose yourself to the outside world's influences. If your reason for participating is to stay connected with friends and like-minded folks, platforms such as Facebook may be good for you. But beware, once you smash POST, and unless you limit who has access to your musings, the whole world can rummage through your life.

I am only on FB to garner best wishes on my Birthday. Well, not really. I am comfortable enough with my skin to share just about everything I do, both in public and private.

The following FB postings are a solid example.

My friends on FB are carefully chosen. I can share my observations, wry sense of humor, and emotions. Emotions that I've held inside to the point of despair. In all that, many have been there for me.

Many have also been there as I've fumbled, stumbled, and regrouped, trying to craft my book on suicide. Those I've chosen to be readers are fantastic at adding comments, observations, and, sometimes, highly charged emotional responses to my story.

2023 passes in a few months, and there are things I need to let go of or put away until I can better cope with the reality that some things are forever.

A friend gave me a plaque years ago that read:

The best things in life aren't things!

Keeping that in mind, I came to these poems as I rewrote the section on the benefits and drawbacks of using social media to maintain contact with others.

As often happens, I am most creative in the early fog of waking up. And I was struck by a desire to write a poem to showcase on **movetothelight.com**. A poem surfacing daily struggles, dashing some plans, yet offering hope for a fulfilling future.

Move to the Light

Have you ever felt abandoned
Do the walls keep closing in
Are your days a mighty struggle
And your nights where demons win
Was it war and all its tragedies
Did a friend fall into the dust
Or your leaders give you orders
Causing moral confusion and mistrust
Did you say that when you grow up
There's a job you've got to have
Answering fire alarms like Uncle Jimmy
Or protecting life the same as dad
I've been told that docs and dentists
Have bad days like you and me
Where the hope they tried to offer
Produced further death and misery
Is there any job worth having
Any friend who's always there
Is the darkness so pervasive
You give in to your despair
Do you hide your pain and anguish
Lashing out, using pills, or maybe booze
Every day a vicious circle
No good answers left to choose
I'm living proof a plan awaits you
No quick fix; the road is long
All it takes is your commitment
And accepting something's wrong
Just as combat boots come in sizes
And hard hats protect your brain
There are therapies and counseling
To set you back on track again

HE's reaching out to those who suffer
Take HIS hand and hold on tight
Life's worth living in all its richness
Together, let us *Move to the Light*!

By Arn Manella

###

Now that you know I like to write poetry, let me share a few with a storyline.

I attended the same grammar school as my dad's family. We all lived on Fairfield Avenue in Chicago, and Lafayette Elementary is only one block away. No busing for us kids. It was in fifth grade when the Chicago Public Schools sponsored a jingle contest. The city sought snappy words to catch the public's interest in revitalizing the city and some neighborhoods. I won with this entry:

Clean up!
Paint up!
Light up!
Make our city gleam!

###

Vietnam is a whole other story. So I won't go into the darker pieces, but rather this sentiment about my situation.

The monsoon here
It's mighty clear
Has one thing on its mind
Invade my clothes
Dilute my beer
And keep me in a bind

The last one, I promise.

Please note, when I write "birth father," that's who I descend from. When I write "dad," that's the man who raised, adopted, and loved Mom and me.

In my life, the one constant is my mother. Mom was always there for my brother and me, but I knew she loved me best. Just kidding. My mom met my dad when she was ten years his junior. When WWII started, my mom traveled to every US Army training station to which dad was assigned. Illinois, Michigan, and Georgia before he shipped out for Iceland.

On the day the telegram arrived to inform Dad's family he is missing in action and presumed dead, Mom is inconsolable, and she departs Chicago for her family living in Kenosha, Wisconsin. The year is 1944.

My birth father is home from the US Navy. They married a few weeks later.

In April 1945, my dad's family was notified he'd been liberated from a German POW camp. My mom tells my birth father she still loves dad, and he begins beating her. I was born in May 1945.

Before he can beat her again, my mom shoots him several times with a 22. cal rifle. He survives, and they are divorced shortly thereafter. In 1971, his family was notified he had died in a Federal prison in California.

My dad and mom live to be eighty years old at my house in California. Mom survives nearly precisely ten years after Dad dies. During that decade, I would call Mom from wherever I was stationed just to check-in. On almost every occasion, Mom answers with, "What do you want?" and then hangs up. But on calls where I quickly say," Mom, I need to talk with you." There is a moment of silence then Mom says," Sweetheart, tell Mom what's wrong."

Remember, I told you. Mom followed my dad to all his training stations before he left. Here's what she did when I told her I was leaving for Vietnam.

My mom doesn't like to fly. She takes trains instead. One day, I was standing phone watch at my Camp Pendleton, California, Staging Unit. The phone rings, and I answer, "Staging battalion, Unit 173, Lance Corporal Manella; how can I help you, sir or mam?" Identifying himself as the Aide to the Commanding General, the caller says the CG wants L/Cpl Manella in his office ASAP. I hand the phone to the Sergeant of the Guard, who responds, "Yes, sir." I'm relieved of duty and ordered to HQ and the CG's Office. I do not know what's going on. The Aide takes me into the CG's office, and my mom sits smiling as I enter. After informing me that he finds my mom quite persuasive, he grants me five days' leave, and I can take up to three other Marines. Walking out of the HQ, my mom says the CG is very friendly. After she told him about Dad's ordeal in WWII and that she wouldn't miss the opportunity to say goodbye to me before I went off to combat, he said he completely understood.

I miss my mom. I am holding her hand when she breathes her last. My brother is also in the room. Once the nurses usher us out, I stoically walk into a small garden area enclosed on all four sides by concrete walls. I start blubbering just like a baby. "Mom...oh mom...please don't leave me...please!"

That afternoon, I drove into the hills above San Clemente to a secluded spot where I could look out over the beautiful blue ocean, and I wrote this:

Last Night I Met an Angel

Last night I met an Angel
As I tossed and turned and sweat
I worried about the things to do
Those completed, those not yet
Where were all the papers
Insurance, car, and such
What bills had been forgotten
Make a total, see how much
The calls, at first a trickle
Soon became a deluge in my ears
Every story and remembrance
Bringing laughter, leaving tears
The Angel, bright eyes shining
Said, slow down; I've things to tell
Don't let your search for answers
Or what needs doing a living Hell

Sudden calmness came upon me
As the Sun's warmth dried my face
I'd found my solid center
In HIS wisdom and HIS Grace
Again, I looked upon her face
Bright eyes shining, ever calm
She smiled, and then I realized
That Angel was my Mom

By remaining on the go and committed to meeting my obligations, I do my best to thwart the devil's efforts to drag me down into the abyss of depression and anxiety. However, I must remain vigilant because I'm often moments away from passive, if not active suicidal ideation.

Chapter 11
Conclusion? - *NO!* It's Just the Beginning

I began my story by stating that I am 90% disabled for combat-related PTSD and related Obstructive Sleep Apnea (OSA) and Totally Disabled and Individually Unemployable (TDIU). I also described how Eddie's mom's question haunted me, asking, "Why not you?"

Four years ago, I found myself hovering between life and death. I chose life; this book tells how I have turned the corner by using every avenue available.

It hasn't been easy, but I can see my way forward with much help from family, friends, and excellent mental health and primary care professionals at the VA.

I am not traveling alone; my goal is to convince others there is hope for, if not a complete cure, that remission from a desire to give in to the dark side is attainable.

I have spent many hours speaking with others informally about suicide. Their support, positive reaction, and encouragement motivated me to write this book. The time spent researching, experimenting with myself, and consulting with mental health practitioners culminated in this final analysis.

What you eat does have a profound impact on your mental health and physical well-being. The medical field is slowly realizing they may be the problem by disregarding metabolic health in favor of a pill for every cure, and the powerful pharmaceutical companies are egging them on.

Another realization is that the number of mental health clinicians available to assist veterans and the public is critically in short supply. I have decided to do my part, and I approached the Veterans Readiness and Education (VR&E) services requesting approval to enter the College of William and Mary M. Ed in Counseling Program. The program has a specific track to aid active-duty military and veterans.

My initial session with the VR&E Counselor was going great until she read in my medical file that not only am I 90% physically disabled, but I am psychologically Totally Disabled and Individually Unemployable (TDIU, which pays at the 100% rate). That disqualifies me from the degree program because it ultimately leads to employment. The only remedy is for me to relinquish my TDIU determination.

Without hesitation, I agreed, and she was stunned. She stated that in her entire career with the VA, no one has ever decided to relinquish their benefits. I told her that it's never about the money. Helping fellow veterans in crisis is priceless.

Lastly, it's taken me five decades to realize that Eddie's mom wasn't accusatory when she said, "Why not you?"

Eddie and I often wrote home about what we would do after we returned from Vietnam. Finish our degrees, become commissioned officers, buy our dream car, and marry the right woman.

I believe Eddie's mom was saying, "Why don't you go on and live Eddie's dream? Make your life a tribute to him and make us all proud."

Eddie, I'm dedicating my continued life to you. I love you, brother. Semper Fi!

Appendix

Chapter 3: NEXUS Letter

June 7, 2020

Veteran: Arnold Nickie Manella

Veteran's SSAN:

To Whom It May Concern,

I am writing this letter in support of Arnold Manella. During my last eight years on active duty, I served as senior medical officer for BUPERS, reviewing all cases and going to the Physical Evaluation Board (PEB) before submission. Additional qualifications and certifications are highlighted below.

I reviewed the veteran's medical discharge from the Marine Corps, dated March 1988. In addition, VAMC Hunter-Holmes McGuire's psychological evaluations and consultations written in 2020 and preceding years and lay testimony are presented in references 1 to 8. And lastly, from my knowledge and frequent observation of the member.

Based on this information, I came to the following conclusion:

Because of his years in the Marines, he developed the following traits which require ongoing treatment:

Member has an occupational and social impairment, with deficiencies in most areas,

   1. Work, family relations, social relation

2. Mood, due to such symptoms as suicidal ideation; (Finally accepted help after years of denial)
3. Near-continuous panic or depression affecting impaired impulse control (such as unprovoked irritability with periods of violence);
4. Difficulty in adapting to stressful circumstances (including work or a work-like setting);
5. Inability to establish and maintain effective relationships at work and with family and friends.

My professional opinion is that his inability to hold meaningful employment since retirement from active military service is more likely than not directly connected to his existing combat-related PTSD.

Since my retirement from active duty, I have served as an instructor for advanced trauma life support for the American College of Surgeons and ▉▉▉▉▉▉▉▉▉▉▉▉▉▉ In addition, I serve on staff in the emergency department ▉▉▉▉▉▉▉▉▉▉▉▉▉▉▉▉. Frank

MD FACEP CAPT(ret) MC USN

C&P Exam ---excerpt----------
--- 2 LOCAL TITLE: C&P EXAMINATION ▉▉▉▉▉▉▉▉▉▉▉▉▉▉▉▉
▉▉▉▉▉▉▉▉▉▉ AUTHOR: ▉▉▉▉ JOHN ▉▉▉▉
▉▉▉ STATUS: COMPLETED Addendum / Clarification Disability Benefits Questionnaire Name of patient/Veteran: Manella, Arnold Nickie ▉▉▉▉▉▉ Veterans electronic folder in VBMS and his treatment notes in CPRS were reviewed. In his C&P of 6/30/20, veteran described having a series of part time positions, and said that if these were made full time, his temperament and behavior would have resulted in him being

163

fired or otherwise losing that job. HE did not indicate he wanted any of those positions to be full time. He reported conflicts regarding how he exposed fraud or other unethical practices and suffered repercussions as a result. However the sum total of his temperament and behavior was consistently described as preventing him from maintaining a job on a full time basis. Treatment notes from ███████████ dated 7/10/20, indicate veterans thought processes were more impaired and his insight into the effects of his behavior on others was impaired to the point of being distorted in two directions. One limiting his awareness of how his behavior was viewed by other people, and the other being the pattern of rigid and catastrophic thinking that would lead him to behaviors that others would find more assaultive than he was able to comprehend. *** Session Duration:60 mins Session Type: Individual Diagnosis: Posttraumatic Stress Disorder (PTSD) Demographic information has been verified and is up to date. Veteran's Goals for Treatment: "Come to terms with what I've missed out on, the should have/ could have's." Discussion: He recently was awarded an increase in sc for PTSD, currently 70%. He reflected on the past and his experiences in Vietnam that he had forgotten until applying for benefits. He continues to struggle with thoughts about being responsible, although he is able to realize he is not completely responsible for certain events and others choices. Cont focusing on building self-awareness of current thought patterns and behaviors. Assessment: Mood: self-contemplative, reflective Thought process: within normal limits Affect: labile Speech: normal rate and tone Judgment: fair Insight: fair No reported change in SI/HI Plan: Continue individual psychotherapy in two weeks. D/c CPT. was impaired to the point of being distorted in two directions. One limiting his awareness of how his behavior was viewed by other people, and the other being the pattern of rigid and

catastrophic thinking that would lead him to behaviors that others would find more assaultive than he was 3 able to comprehend. Veterans long term pattern of offensive and frightening behavior stands apart from the retributions he experienced as a result of his reactions to unethical behaviors and reflects the degree to which he has been unable to maintain a full time, steady position and his pattern of part time jobs was not a choice or preference as much as it was a natural reaction to his inability to maintain a full time job due to the behavior patterns described in his observations, those listed in his C&P of 6/30/20, and those described in his therapy notes. . /es/ JOHN███████████STAFF PSYCHOLOGIST --excerpt---------
----

Chapter 5:

In a **Lexipol** study by **Karen Lansing** in 2006, Marines, Army, and National Guard forces activated downrange were assessed. First, the soldiers are screened regarding their psychological status (i.e., levels of PTSD, depression, and anxiety present). Next, soldiers answered 17 questions that assessed whether their leaders were high or low in positive leadership skills. The study evaluated all combat levels (mild, moderate, and extreme).

Within the Marines, teams operating in consistently high levels of combat engagement and rated their leaders as "high" in positive leadership skills had a 19 percent incidence of psychological hardship (e.g., PTSD, depression, anxiety). For those who rated their leaders as "low" in positive leadership skills, the incidence of psychological hardship rose to 44 percent. These trends were consistent across the three military branches and repeated in subsequent assessments among Law Enforcement, Fire, and First Responder communities.

"*That's a staggering spread*," Lansing says, "but it reflects the largest obstacle I encounter in my work. *"The biggest problem I have when treating duty-induced PTSD isn't with neutralizing the event and facilitating the opportunity for adaptive learning for the first responder. I can take care of that very easily. But if I 4 encounter trauma after the event rendered due to poor leadership, I may never be able to bring their officer back."* She has helped return fully to the job in all of the hundreds after treating their PTSD; there are nine who Lansing could not return, six in one law enforcement agency and three in another. *"These were very troubled agencies and lost all nine due to this leadership issue,"* Lansing says.

https://www.lexipol.com/resources/blog/post-traumatic-stress-disorder-law-enforcement-officers/

"The USMC Oscar Gen III is designed to provide selected Marines, sailors, medical professionals, religious ministry teams, and mental health professionals with the information and resources needed to help Marines and sailors prevent, identify, and manage combat and operational stress issues early as possible before they become medical problems."

That was nearly 50 years ago. I am happy to report that the Marine Corps is rapidly catching up with the times by recognizing the vagaries brought upon by combat and stress, with proper implementation of recognized neuro-physiological programs.

###

Reluctance to label the death of a veteran, LEO, or first responder as a suicide can be based on the concern that any benefits due will be withheld. Examples include life insurance policies with a suicide clause voiding any payout within the first two years of the policy coming into force. The recently passed **Public Safety Officers Benefits (PSOB) Program** provided death and education benefits to survivors of fallen enforcement officers, firefighters, and other first responders and disability benefits to officers catastrophically injured in the line of duty.

Chapter 7:

In Credible Catholic, Presentation 1, CHAPTER 1, **Proof of a Soul and Heaven from Near-Death Experiences (NDEs)**, there are five NDE studies from medical professionals and scientists that highlight their observations of their patients, each of which is eye-opening and cause for the belief we do have a transcendent soul. I am particularly interested in the interview by Dr. Raymond Moody with Dr. Bruce Greyson, then of the University of Virginia. Dr. Greyson has been studying NDEs for over 30 years. He has been called the "Father of Near-Death Experience Research."

Dr. Greyson described the change he noticed in many of his patients as a result of their NDEs, saying:

- "They lose their fear of living life to the fullest because they are not afraid of taking chances anymore. They're not afraid of dying. So they get more interested in life and enjoy it much more than they did before."

In answer to a question by Dr. Moody as to if people that made suicide attempts and had an NDE as a result, "When they recover do they have a desire to commit suicide?" Dr. Greyson answers,

- "They do not! Patients are saying they no longer are considering suicide as an option. Usually, because they see their problem in a different perspective, they no longer identify with this bag of skin. They think of something greater than themselves. Their problems are not enough to end this life."

Dr. Greyson continues,

- "They see a sense of meaning and purpose they didn't see before. They recount seeing others, relatives, friends, angels, and some even God. They describe this warm, loving being of Light. All over the world and here in North America, they might often call that God, Christ, or something of a religious nature. In other cultures, they may not use the same words; rather, acceptance, unconditional 3 6 love. Death is not the end; the consciousness (read: Soul...my word) continues." © Magis Center 2017

On one of my long driving trips, I listened to Dr. Grayson, who mentioned that a person might be under the effect of an NDE from seconds to less than a minute. But when asked to describe their experiences, a patient can go on from several minutes up to an hour because there isn't a relationship between time as we understand it and time as it happened.

Chapter 8: Week One of my Lenten Makeover

Well, it has been a week since I began this five days ago on Ash Wednesday, but it serves as a baseline for physical condition, setting the areas to be considered and results.

Here are the results:

Alcohol: I was drinking two glasses of wine with dinner daily. Occasionally, I would sit in my backyard on lovely days and have one or two Gin and diet tonics in the afternoon. Sundays, with my pound of shrimp, I'd have one glass of white wine. 11 **Result:** I have had no alcohol. I miss the taste, but when I grab a Pellegrino, it satisfies my "grab and drink" at meals. My mind is clear, and I am sleeping well. **Beginner Bodyweight program.** I am doing the four circuits on Mondays, Wednesdays, and Fridays. All six exercises are difficult—push-ups especially. Plank, side straddle hops, hip raise, lunge, and squats are doable, but the technique needs to be improved.

Result: I am a bit sore, and my muscles are tight, but all good.

BBBE: Eating beef, butter, bacon, and eggs is not difficult, and I enjoy it. But, I find myself craving sweets at Church on Sundays, where we have hospitality after Mass, and there are always donuts, cookies, and pastries. But I'm holding my own.

Result: My weight is down from 217 to 212 this morning.

One Meal a Day (OMAD). Also not a problem. When I do have two meals, it's within four hours.

Result: interval fasting is also aiding with weight loss and providing energy to my body and brain.

Five-day water-only fast. Due to First Friday Mass, where the region has a breakfast meeting, I will postpone the fast until Saturday (3-4) morning and conclude on Thursday morning (3-9).

Second Monday of my Lenten Makeover

Alcohol: None since Ash Wednesday

Result: I continue to miss the taste, but then it might be a force of habit where I grab wine at dinner or G & T. My mind remains clear, sleeping well, and I've noticed an enhanced ability to detect smells. For example, a friend poured himself a bourbon across the room. I could detect it immediately. And, in a crowded room, the pleasant essence of perfume and unpleasant odor of, well, you can guess, was apparent.

Beginner Bodyweight program. I am doing the four circuits, but the days change due to circumstances beyond my control. However, all six exercises are getting better as my technique improves.

Result: I am less sore, and my muscles are tight, but all good.

BBBE: Eating beef, butter, bacon, and eggs is missed.

Result: My weight is down from 212 to 205 this morning.

One Meal a Day (OMAD). Resumes tomorrow. I have not been hungry at all. However, I'm surrounded by food.

Result: Holding my own.

Five-day water-only fast*: Knowing I would attend several events, one on Friday with Breakfast, one on Saturday with dinner, and one on Sunday with Lunch with pizza, I started my fast on Thursday at 10 am.

Result: As you can see by my weight, the loss of seven pounds is pretty good. I can't attribute it all to water weight loss because my weight from Ash Wednesday to the first Monday was a pound a day, and this seven-day period is also a pound a day. All VERY good.

*Ok, today I broke my five-day water-only fast.

Doing more than jumping into your usual daily meal selection would be best. Usually, I only eat One Meal A Day, but you will see that if I go right to the meal, I will lay out. This is because I could quickly put myself at risk of severe side effects. Your digestive system (from mouth to anus) undergoes several fundamental changes. For example, your throat may feel constricted, your stomach may be uneasy, and the bacteria in your digestive tract (intestines) not be at peak performance levels. Consequently, I must ease into it.

Here is how today's regime went to break my fast and return my microbiome to full functioning.

Once I got up, I took two teaspoons of Extra Virgin Olive Oil.

Two hours before my first "meal," I ate one egg over easy and a half cup of Sauerkraut. Sauerkraut is fermented cabbage and a good source of live and active cultures that support the microbiome, and in the right amount is likely better than probiotic supplements.

The meal: a plate of Italian sausage with grilled peppers and onions and a second plate with meatballs, peppers, and onions. Two glasses of unsweetened iced tea. I am home now, and for a final heavy snack: 1/4-pound braunschweiger, avocado, and water.

It will be interesting to see my weight following Monday following my return to the Ketovore lifestyle. Up to this point, I've been losing a pound a day. I weighed in at 205 Monday.

Third Monday of my Lenten Makeover

No alcohol: Going great! No desire to drink this week. Pellegrino sparkling water is refreshing. I add electrolytes and Iodine. On occasion, I will add Apple Cider Vinegar. It tastes delicious and is excellent for the microbiome.

Body Workout. I am chugging along. I haven't increased the reps but it is easier each time.

BBBE. I have a confession: I attended a Retreat here at St Timothy this Lent. The Retreat leader is Father Jonathan, formerly our pastor and currently the pastor at Our Lady of Lourdes. That was the upside. The downside was that someone baked fresh nibbles (Danish), and I ate three over the four-hour presentation. **The result**: my weight this morning is 208. You may remember my weight last Monday was 205. So why the change? I have these theories, and I don't mean the Danish. 1. It was mostly water weight. Monday was the last full day of the five-day water-only fast. Consequently, there's a good chance the significant drop was partially water loss, not fat. 2. I gained a pound because of muscle growth. I like this one. A more accurate indicator is my waist size. Before this, I was very comfortable wearing size 38 trousers. I could squeeze into the 36, but it was uncomfortable. This morning I am wearing 36 and feel great.

OMAD. To increase my protein intake and support my weight training, I have eaten an additional meal within four hours of dinner. This usually consists of four eggs over-easy, Sauerkraut, and bacon.

Fourth Monday of my Lenten Makeover

Alcohol: St Patrick's Day found me at a celebration at St Patrick's Church in Lexington, VA. Father Stefan is a long-time friend, and his parish is celebrating 150 years in the valley. Celebrating the Mass is our Bishop Barry Knestow. After Mass, the Bishop gave everyone a dispensation of their Lenten Penances. I started at the Virginia Military Institute (VMI) Hall of Heroes with a small G&T, a 2-ounce glass of red and white wine (not mixed). Next, I ate a hefty slice of red meat, a large piece of chicken parmesan, and a birthday cake.

Result: I'm satiated by the food with little effect from the alcohol. I was just as happy drinking water with the remainder of the meal. I didn't expect that to be the case.

Beginner Bodyweight program. I am doing the four circuits, but the days continue to change due to circumstances beyond my control. However, all six exercises are getting better as my technique improves.

Result: I am doing fine.

BBBE. Eating beef, butter, bacon, and eggs remains my meal staple. However, after I ate a corner piece of the birthday cake, I noticed I had a craving for sugar for the next few days.

Result: My weight is 204 this morning, and my size 36 trousers threaten to fall unless I tighten my belt another notch.

One Meal a Day (OMAD). Remaining the standard, though three times this week, I did eat four-six eggs, Sauerkraut, and bacon four hours before my evening meal. **Result:** Feeling good.

Five-day water-only fast. Knowing I would attend the St Patrick's Day celebration, I followed up with a 72-hour water-only fast. That ends at 2 pm today.

Fifth Monday of Lenten Makeover

Alcohol: None.

Result: clearer of mind, no craving, but as the weather improves and I can sit in the backyard, a nice G&T would hit the spot. That said, no desire for wine with supper. **Bodywork Out**: three times a week

Result: easier up the stairs and bending improves

BBBE: easy to maintain.

Result: no body aches, stiff joints, sleep well—weight 211, up from 204

No fasting. I returned to soccer this past weekend. Quite a bit of walking. So, why did the weight increase? I am eating three meals a day, rather than normal OMAD. I eat the usual beef, butter, bacon, and eggs, but with the timing of meals off Breakfast at 0630, Lunch at 1230, and supper at 1930...my digestion is off kilter. This coming weekend is part 2 of the soccer tournament, so I expect my weight to remain the same.

The Sixth Monday of my Lenten Makeover

Lent officially ends on Holy Thursday, three days from today. But as can happen, circumstances can intrude on the best plan. There is an agreement in most addiction programs that if the addict can go 30 days without returning to the drug of choice, they stand a better than even chance of breaking the bad habit. My drugs of choice are chocolate (sugar) and alcohol. I've already reported that I enjoyed both three weeks in and now again this past Friday.

Although I've brought my dopamine baseline higher and did not need either drug, I didn't factor in the need for a" high" after losing an acquaintance. Although I didn't drink any alcohol, that night, I did eat 4 Baklava. The result is an immediate insulin spike. I couldn't sleep, and severe aches and pains for the next two days. Saturday at the farm, I had a G&T. I had a glass of wine last night. It didn't taste all that good. So, what's the current report?

Alcohol: One glass of white wine and a G&T.

Result: No desire for more, but emotions can move very quickly.

Body workout: No increase in reps or appreciable change. I'm going to keep stretching and alternate with walking.

Result: Feel fine.

BBBE remains the standard regime.

Result: All is good when I don't eat off the menu. Weight this AM 207

Seventh Monday of my Lenten Makeover

Happy Easter, my friends.

Alcohol: Well, I thought I'd jump off the wagon and return to alcohol as my drug of choice, but NO. I had one glass of wine after Vigil Mass Saturday, a G&T, and one glass of wine on Sunday at my daughter's for Easter dinner. After that, several glasses of water before bed. In the past, it's been alcohol that sent me to sleep, but maybe that's no longer the case.

Result: Within 24 hours of consumption, although not feeling foggy, I could tell I wasn't 100 %. But that's about all. Let's monitor over the next few weeks. I start teaching sailing again this coming weekend. In the past, I felt like I needed alcohol to relax after sailing all day.

Body workout: No increase in reps or 16 appreciable change. It's evident that muscle mass is increasing, and walking is very relaxing. The dogs like it.

Result: I feel terrific and quite happy mentally.

BBBE: proved to be a big success overall. I did a water-only fast from Tuesday afternoon to Saturday afternoon to close out Lentand honor Our Lord's crucifixion, death, and resurrection.

Result: The belt I was wearing I purchased a year ago started at 42in and went down to 37in. I now have a new belt that begins at 36in. Let's see where that goes—weight this AM 204 lbs.

ABOUT THE AUTHOR
Arnold "Arn" Manella

Arn was born in Libertyville, Illinois, in 1945 to Scot/Welsh and Belgian parents. His birth father, who recently returned from service with the US Navy in the Pacific, often beat his mother. The beatings were likely due to two key factors: 1. His aircraft carrier survived many Japanese attacks, and he lost many good friends consequently, he may have suffered from PTSD, and 2. Upon receiving word that her "true love," thought to have been killed in Germany, was repatriated from a POW camp, his mother asked for a divorce. Once the divorce is final, she remarries for love. Moving to Chicago, Arn's family is increased by a brother.

Arn initially did well in school until sixth grade, when he suffered a TBI falling from a moving car. As a result, his ability to focus suffers. Still, he does well enough to the letter in high school and college sports, receiving numerous awards for leadership.

The advent of the Vietnam War finds Arn in the US Marines, where he and his new best Marine buddy Eddie become fast friends. Unfortunately, Eddie is KIA just ten days before his return from Vietnam. That singular event begins Arn's free-fall toward combat-related PTSD, exacerbated by his assignments over the next twenty-plus years on active duty. Additionally, betrayal by a close friend results in Arn's divorce from his fabulous wife—the mother of their two fantastic children. She died of ovarian cancer at the young age of fifty-two.

For the next three decades, Arn's attempt to adjust to a civilian career is hampered by his inability to bend when faced with superiors motivated by profit and advancement over moral leadership.

Finally accepting that the problem is likely more profound, Arn turns to the Veterans Administration. Initially, the diagnosis is mild PTSD, with treatment running the gambit from Tai Chi to drugs—his reliance on medication results in a loss of motivation and an inability to focus critically or continue professional writing.

In February 2020, Arn stood before Eddie's name on the Vietnam Veterans Memorial, better known as 'the Wall." Haunted by Eddie's mom asking at the funeral, "Why not you?" Arn drives back to his Virginia farm and plans how he'll commit suicide, yet leave the impression it's but a terrible accident.

Recognizing that suicide is not the answer, Arn begins a rigorous remaking of his life. He returns to the VA medical center for clinical treatment. He successfully negotiates the minefield of the Veterans Benefits Administration for the benefits he's earned and to God to see him through it all.

Today, Arn has decided to live a long time, and he wants to share his journey revealing "how he" is negotiating the many speed bumps and potholes that continue to hamper a safe exit from the active suicidal ideation highway toward his ultimate destination of living a happy, healthy, and fulfilled life.

You can reach out to Arn at:
suicideandthe90daywindow@gmail.com

Made in the USA
Middletown, DE
15 October 2023

40773640R00108